Forward to Freedom

Forward to Freedom

A Journey into God

DAVID ADAM

First published in 1999 by
Darton, Longman and Todd Ltd
1 Spencer Court
140–142 Wandsworth High Street
London SW18 4JJ

ISBN 0-232-52324-X

A catalogue record for this book is available
from the British Library.

Designed by Sandie Boccacci
Phototypeset in New Century Schoolbook by
Intype London Ltd
Printed and bound in Great Britain by
Redwood Books, Trowbridge, Wiltshire

Contents

Introduction

In Bede's *Life of Cuthbert*, Chapter Eight on the death of Saint Boisil begins with the words, 'The whole state of the world is frail and unstable as the sea when a sudden tempest arises': we, as we enter the third millennium, know this as well as any generation. It seems that there are ever wars and rumours of wars, peoples are crying to be freed from captivity and longing for the Promised Land; rules are being made and broken, many are perishing in the wilderness, too many are looking back and are afraid to move forward.

A good book for our times is the Book of Exodus. It will encourage us to come out of our captivities and perhaps even help to bring others to freedom: from Exodus we will hear God saying, 'Tell the people to go forward'. The Exodus is about God hearing the cry of his people and meeting their every need, about God binding himself to this small nation by covenant. We discover how a relationship with God affects the way people live and when they break that relationship how God acts in grace. Here we will learn that God calls us out and calls us forward to freedom. The journey from slavery to freedom is a forty-year journey; it takes a lifetime. As long as we live, this journey into freedom is as important to each of us as it was to the children of Israel. The Exodus can reveal to us so much about our own position, attitudes and pilgrimage that it is worth a deep study. This is a journey through the wilderness of this world in the presence of our God. It is not just about a race of people from the past, it is about you and your journey through life. What do you do when faced with weakness or a lack of power? Where do you turn when your resources run out? Learn how a people travelled through darkness and desert and came into freedom. See how their faith grows and how God asks allegiance of them.

Once when I was telling a very dramatic Bible story to a group of children, I had just arrived at the exciting part when a child interrupted, 'Am I in that story? Am I in that story?' I nodded, and hoped to continue, but he persisted? 'Am I a goody or a baddy? What will I do?' At the time I could only stop and help him decide where he stood in relation to the story. Later, I realised that this little lad had given me the most wonderful insight into Bible study. No longer could I wallow in theological theories, or spend hours arguing on dates; I had to ask 'Am I in that story?' and 'What will I do?' In looking at the story of Exodus, I want to look at it from where we are today and what it asks of us. I am interested in history, but I am more interested in what today leads us into the ways of peace, what helps us to behold the glory of God. Let us see the Exodus as God's call to us to move from where we are and nearer to the Promised Land. It is a call to commitment and obedience as well as a call to glory. It was St John Chrysostom who said, 'It is not enough to leave Egypt, one must also enter the Promised Land.' In our age we demand freedom and rightly so, but freedom to do what and to go where? There is a great joy for all those who discover that his service is perfect freedom.

When Saint Boisil had only seven days to live and was unable to go out, he said that Cuthbert should make this an opportunity of learning. Boisil said he had a copy of the Gospel according to Saint John in seven separately stitched sections and, with the Lord's help, they would read it and discuss it between themselves. Bede says, 'They were able to finish the reading because they dealt only with the simple things of the faith inspired by love and not matters of deep dispute.' I intend this to be my approach to the Book of Exodus. I will not argue about dates or the location of some of the events, or even when different parts of the book were written. I will seek, with the Lord's help, to deal with the simple things of the faith and not enter into deep dispute. I will use the forty days of Lent as the basis for forty sections, and at the end of each section there will be a prayer, for we are not so much the people of the Book as the people of God. I believe that God still comes to us, and calls us; he has a purpose for us and seeks to lead us forward to freedom. I have added a reading for Easter Day, as we rejoice in him who has rescued us and redeemed us, freeing us from the slavery of sin and death, and opened for us the gate of glory.

1

Is My Name There?

These are the names of the sons of Israel who went with Jacob to Egypt, each with his family: • *Reuben, Simeon, Levi and Judah,* • *Issachar, Zebulun and Benjamin,* • *Dan and Naphtali, Gad and Asher.* • *In all, the descendants of Jacob numbered seventy persons. Joseph was in Egypt already.* • *Then Joseph died, and his brothers, and all that generation.* • *But the sons of Israel were fruitful and grew in numbers greatly; they increased and grew so immensely powerful that they filled the land.*

Then there came to power in Egypt a new king who knew nothing of Joseph. 'Look,' he said to his subjects 'these people, the sons of Israel, have become so numerous and strong that they are a threat to us. • *We must be prudent and take steps against their increasing any further, or if war should break out, they might add to the number of our enemies. They might take arms against us and so escape out of the country.' • Accordingly they put slave-drivers over the Israelites to wear them down under heavy loads. In this way they built the store-cities of Pithom and Rameses for Pharaoh.* • *But the more they were crushed, the more they increased and spread, and men came to dread the sons of Israel.* • *The Egyptians forced the sons of Israel into slavery,* • *and made their lives unbearable with hard labour, work with clay and with brick, all kinds of work in the fields; they forced on them every kind of labour.*

Exodus 1:1–14

In the Hebrew language the Book of Exodus is called after its first word, 'Shemot', which is 'Names'. The listing of the names of Jacob's family (1:1–6) is to let us know that this is a follow-on from the stories in the Book of Genesis: in a sense it begins where Genesis left off, with the Hebrews who entered

Egypt because of Joseph. This is the continuing story of the twelve tribes of Israel, the story of the people of God. We must remember, as this story was told, its listeners would relate to a member or members of these families. It is the story of their ancestors without whom they would not have come into existence: they might have said they belonged to the 'House of Levi' or to the 'Little tribe of Benjamin'. Even people who were not direct ancestors were distant uncles and all had names and stories attached to them. They might be the twelve tribes of Israel, but they were individuals with distinct personalities.

I find it hard to say when I was first attracted to Christianity, but one moment of importance goes back to my childhood and my uncle Bob. My uncle was a soldier in the Second World War and towards the end of the war he came home on a short leave. When I talked with him, he showed me his army-issue New Testament, it had a khaki cover and fitted neatly into his battledress pocket. Inside, on the flyleaf of this book, was printed 'God so loved . . . . that he gave his only begotten son, that whosoever believes in him should not perish but have everlasting life' (John 3:16). I asked my uncle why there was a gap and he replied, 'To put your name in'. My uncle had not bothered so it was still blank. I was so fascinated by this text and the ability to put your name into it that my uncle gave it to me. I carefully wrote my name in my best writing, for it was a moment of great discovery. 'God so loved David Adam': he actually cared about me as a person. Until that moment I did not realise that God knew me at all.

Much later, I would thrill to hear the words 'But now, thus says Yahweh, who created you, Jacob, who formed you, Israel: Do not be afraid, for I have redeemed you; I have called you by your name, you are mine. Should you pass through the sea, I will be with you; or through rivers, they will not swallow you up. Should you walk through fire, you will not be scorched and the flames will not burn you. For I am Yahweh, your God, the Holy One of Israel, your saviour' (Isaiah 43:1–3).

These words can easily describe the travels and adventures of Moses or they can fit your own life. Take your time reading over this passage of Isaiah and put your name there: in the reading replace the words 'Jacob' and 'Israel' with your own name. Know that God speaks to you and calls you by your name. Perhaps, for you, this will be the first movement out of captivity and into the glorious liberty of the children of God.

Now write out John 3:16 and put your name where it says 'the world'. Know that you are loved by God and you are in the very heart of God. God cares for you and the place you are in.

Holy God, Holy and Strong One, Holy and Mighty One,
we give thanks that you have called us by our name.
Open our ears to your call, open our hearts to your love,
that we may walk with confidence, obeying your will,
    abiding in your presence
and rejoicing in your love for us.

2

Born Free

The king of Egypt then spoke to the Hebrew midwives, one of whom was named Shiphrah, and the other Puah. • 'When you midwives attend Hebrew women,' he said 'watch the two stones carefully. If it is a boy, kill him; if a girl, let her live.' • But the midwives were God-fearing: they disobeyed the command of the king of Egypt and let the boys live. • So the king of Egypt summoned the midwives. 'Why' he asked them 'have you done this and spared the boys?' • 'The Hebrew women are not like Egyptian women,' they answered Pharaoh 'they are hardy, and they give birth before the midwife reaches them.' • God was kind to the midwives. The people went on increasing and grew very powerful; • since the midwives reverenced God he granted them descendants.

Pharaoh then gave his subjects this command: 'Throw all the boys born to the Hebrews into the river, but let all the girls live'.

There was a man of the tribe of Levi who had taken a woman of Levi as his wife. • She conceived and gave birth to a son and, seeing what a fine child he was, she kept him hidden for three months. • When she could hide him no longer, she got a papyrus basket for him; coating it with bitumen and pitch, she put the child inside and laid it among the reeds at the river's edge. • His sister stood some distance away to see what would happen to him.

Now Pharaoh's daughter went down to bathe in the river, and the girls attending her were walking along by the riverside. Among the reeds she noticed the basket, and she sent her maid to fetch it. • She opened it and looked, and saw a baby boy, crying; and she was sorry for him. 'This is a child of one of the Hebrews' she said. • Then the child's sister said to Pharaoh's daughter, 'Shall I go and find you a nurse among the Hebrew women to suckle the child for you?' • 'Yes, go' Pharaoh's daughter said to her; and the girl went off to find the baby's own mother. • To her the daughter of Pharaoh said, 'Take this child away and suckle it for me. I will

4

see you are paid.' So the woman took the child and suckled it. • *When the child grew up, she brought him to Pharaoh's daughter who treated him like a son; she named him Moses because, she said, 'I drew him out of the water'.*

Exodus 1:15–2:10

Life is always changing and we cannot live off past triumphs or past glories for long. As living creatures, if we become static we stagnate and die. Life moves forward and extends itself or it diminishes and moves towards captivity and death. We are born with certain freedoms but they can soon be lost to others or sacrificed for momentary comfort. Sometimes we do not recognise that life has changed and things are no longer as they used to be.

'Then there came to power in Egypt a new king who knew nothing of Joseph.' When the nomadic Hebrews first came into the Nile area of Egypt they must have thought they had arrived in the Garden of Eden. After struggling in drought-stricken Canaan and crossing the desert lands to come to Joseph, the Nile valley must have seemed full of promise. In the land of Goshen they were a privileged group with support from Pharaoh through Joseph; never had they been so well off. Here the children of Israel prospered and increased until 'the land was filled with them'. Here was a case of an ethnic group that was first welcomed but now local people objected to their presence and their privileged position. Suddenly there were exaggerated accounts of how many there were – 'they seem to be everywhere'. What had been a privileged position disappeared. The forced labour that the Hebrews had to perform was probably no different from what other local farmers had to do, but the privileges given to the Hebrews had gone. Somehow they still prospered and the Egyptians continued to complain.

Pharaoh then tried a new stratagem and, in secret, he asked the Hebrew midwives to get rid of all new-born males. Pharaoh would not be the last tyrant to practise infanticide. The mid-wives were 'God fearing' and did not obey Pharaoh, obviously at great risk to themselves. They would not sacrifice their beliefs for security and they had a higher king to whom they owed allegiance. The cunning of Pharaoh was defeated by the artfulness of the midwives. These brave women were called Shiphrah and Puah (1:15); their names mean 'Beauty' and 'Splendour'. They were thinking and feeling women and would not obey blindly. How often tyranny is defeated by those who keep their birthright of beauty and splendour. How often in history women play a strong role in the resistance movement. Evil can only triumph if good refuses to make a stand. Because of the midwives the Hebrew birth-rate was not diminished. Now Pharaoh had to come out into the open and demand the death of every Hebrew male.

No names are given to the parents of Moses until later (see Exodus 6:20 and Numbers 26:59). The sister is also nameless and it is only later tradition that calls her Miriam. It is noted that both of the parents of Moses were of the house of Levi (2:1). That their child was male was a great joy to them but also brought great fear. Would the soldiers hear the baby's cry? How could they hide him for long? For three whole months the mother fed the infant at risk to herself, but she knew this could not continue without being discovered. No doubt his mother decided it was better for the child to be exposed to uncertainty than to certain death. In this life, if we are afraid of un-certainty we will die a thousand deaths and never fully live. So, the child was placed in a little waterproofed reed basket and put in the reeds of the River Nile under the watchful eyes of his sister.

It is interesting to compare the hardness and brutality of Pharaoh with the compassion and gentleness of his daughter. The daughter of Pharaoh realises this is a little Hebrew boy yet she adopts him as her own and gives him an Egyptian name. It is likely that he was called Ahmosis or Thutmosis or some other common Egyptian name. The Hebrew explanation that it means 'drawn out' or 'rescued' is part of the story of God's saving grace. There is something wonderful about the tradition that Moses was then given back to his parents and they were paid for nursing him on behalf of Pharaoh's daughter. Whether we know it or not, at all times God cares for us.

Holy God, protector of the weak, guardian of the outcast,
we remember before you all who are suffering from tyranny
at this time.
We pray for all oppressed peoples and their freedom.
We rejoice that you call us into the glorious liberty of the
children of God;
through Jesus Christ, who died and rose again and who
lives with you and the Holy Spirit, one God, now and
forever. Amen.

3

Pilgrim in a Foreign Land

Moses, a man by now, set out at this time to visit his countrymen, and he saw what a hard life they were having; and he saw an Egyptian strike a Hebrew, one of his countrymen. • *Looking round he could see no one in sight, so he killed the Egyptian and hid him in the sand.* • *On the following day he came back, and there were two Hebrews, fighting. He said to the man who was in the wrong, 'What do you mean by hitting your fellow countryman?'* • *'And who appointed you' the man retorted* • *'to be prince over us, and judge? Do you intend to kill me as you killed the Egyptian?' Moses was frightened. 'Clearly that business has come to light' he thought.* • *When Pharaoh heard of the matter he would have killed Moses, but Moses fled from Pharaoh and made for the land of Midian.* • *And he sat down beside a well.*

Now the priest of Midian had seven daughters. They came to draw water and fill the troughs to water their father's sheep. • *Shepherds came and drove them away, but Moses came to their defence and watered their sheep for them.* • *When they returned to their father Reuel, he said to them, 'You are back early today!' 'An Egyptian protected us from the shepherds;' they said 'yes, and he drew water for us and watered the flock.'* • *'And where is he?' he asked his daughters. 'Why did you leave the man there? Ask him to eat with us.'* • *So Moses settled with this man, who gave him his daughter Zipporah in marriage.* • *She gave birth to a son, and he named him Gershom because, he said, 'I am a stranger in a foreign land'.*

Exodus 2:11–22

The story so far is very like a folk tale and has parallels in other stories of this area. The poor boy who became a prince is a wonderful tale. Now the story takes a turn. If you belong to a people that are oppressed, and you have a position

8

of privilege, then you have a responsibility towards them. In our times those who have any money at all have a responsibility for the world's poor. Again we see that evil will triumph if good people do nothing. It would have been easy for Moses to turn his back on his own people and to enjoy all the delights of the royal court. Moses was in a safe position, as privileged as the Israelites had all been in the time of Joseph, and even better off. Moses 'went out to see his own people and looked on their burdens'. In the New Testament the writer to the Hebrews says, 'he refused to be known as the son of Pharaoh's daughter'. No doubt from his parents he learnt of the suffering of his own people and how they longed for freedom. Now in front of his very eyes he saw an Egyptian beating one of his own people. Something stirred within him, deep feelings and anguish burst out in anger. He killed the Egyptian then buried him in the sand. Now he had made a major move in showing his care for his own: he had come out from his position of safety and was standing up for the oppressed.

The next day, Moses came out again, this time to mediate between two of his own people, and they rejected him. No doubt they were jealous of his position and afraid that if they were associated with him they would be blamed for the killing of the Egyptian. Moses had made a stand but the Hebrews did not want to be moved, they refused his help. So often in history leaders are rejected by the very people they seek to serve. People choose security rather than freedom. It is often easier to accept a lesser way of life and restricted freedom than to risk stepping out and moving towards a greater freedom. There is no joy over Moses rescuing the slaves, only suspicion of his actions. Moses could have helped his people secretly, but now his cover has been destroyed and he is sought by Pharaoh who wants to kill him. At the same time Moses is also rejected by the Hebrew slaves. He is forced to flee into the wilderness to save his life. At least his position at court would allow him to leave the city without being challenged by the guards.

The scene changes and Moses is sitting at a well in the land of Midian. The Midianites were a semi-nomadic people living over a large area in the south of Moab and east of the Gulf of Aqaba – we cannot be certain of the exact area. In this desert region among nomadic shepherds Moses, dressed as a member of the royal court, must have stood out like a sore thumb. He watches as the women draw water from the well. He sees them fill the troughs and then the shepherds seek to drive them away and take the water. Moses intervenes and rescues the women. He draws water for them and waters their sheep. He has moved from one battle about justice to another. The women go and tell their father, Reuel, of their adventure and he asks why they have not brought the man home. Moses accepts with joy and not only receives Bedouin hospitality but is given work. In time he is given a wife, Zipporah. Now we have the years of domesticity and it would seem that all that went before is forgotten and wasted. All of his education and privileged position had been for nothing. Now he was learning to be a shepherd in the semi-desert, to survive in the sandy wastes and to make sure his flock survived also. Now he would learn of ancient roads and trackways. His teacher would be Reuel, 'the shepherd of God', who was also called Jethro and was the priest of Midian.

The meeting of the caring Egyptian and the daughter of Jethro has all the making of romance. Moses calls his first-born 'Gershom', which means 'I have been a stranger in a foreign land'. Was he saying at this point there was still a strange restlessness within him? This time of love and desert training will take Moses a long way.

We are able to see the plight of suffering people and sub-jugated people regularly through television. Do we allow this to move us? If we do not react there must be something in us that has died. With our God, we are asked to stand for justice and freedom.

Lord, you have called us to stand for freedom,
to seek liberty for all peoples,
help us to stand out for justice,
to work for fair dealings
and to seek a glorious liberty for all your children:
    through Jesus Christ our Lord.

4

God Hears and Cares

During this long period the king of Egypt died. The sons of Israel, groaning in their slavery, cried out for help and from the depths of their slavery their cry came up to God. • *God heard their groaning and he called to mind his covenant with Abraham, Isaac and Jacob.* • *God looked down upon the sons of Israel, and he knew . . .*

Exodus 2:23–25

In these brief verses time has passed. The Pharaoh who caused the Hebrews to suffer has died, but their situation is no better. No doubt they had hoped for an improvement in their lot but it was not to be. In their troubles they cry out to God and God hears. This is a pattern that will be found throughout the Old Testament: in good times people forget God, in bad times they call for help. God hears, God remembers his covenant; God sees, God knows and God acts.

It is not that God ever forgets or fails to see, but he waits to be invited. Even now, God is waiting to come and meet us if we will turn to him. Jesus witnesses to this in the story of the Prodigal Son (Luke 15:11–32). See how the father waits for the wayward son and goes out to meet him and to welcome him home. One of my learning points came with the phrase 'Prayers cannot be answered unless they are prayed'. Even if we do not know the right words God heeds our groaning, he hears the innermost sighs and longings and waits to be invited to help.

Sometimes people will not be moved until they recognise how

bad their present condition has become. To make progress it is necessary to give people a vision of a better world and of a loving, caring God; we need to make people realise that they need not be content with restricted lives. People of today are often trapped by subtle forms of slavery and need to be shown a freer, more life-extending way to live. Many are possessed by their possessions and cannot break free. There was a lovely quip by an American who, when asked of a self-made million-aire, 'What did he leave?', said, 'He left it all'. So many people's lives are crammed so full of things and experiences that they have no room for God. Many of us need to experience the emptiness within before we realise that in his love God had made there a place for himself.

To live for experiences alone is like drinking salt water to quench your thirst – you will thirst for more and more. There is something in all of us that knows of the eternal. Augustine says, 'Lord, our hearts are restless until they rest in you.' Very often in all of us there is a groaning and a longing, there is an awareness that we have forgotten our maker.

The Hebrews had moved away from the land of their God to the land of Egypt and its alien gods, and it took them a while to realise that their God went with them. They did not move out of the heart of God. The turning point of their situation is when they realise that they have a God who hears, who remem-bers them and who knows their needs. In this God they can have hope and confidence. God, in his care, has bonded himself to them. God says to us and to them, 'I will never leave you or forsake you'.

> God, you hear our cries before we speak them,
> you know our needs before we see them,
> without you we are poor indeed.
> Come, Lord, come to us,
> refresh us,
> free us and empower us,

that we may become the people you want us to be:
through Jesus Christ our Lord.

5

The Presence

Moses was looking after the flock of Jethro, his father-in-law, priest of
Midian. He led his flock to the far side of the wilderness and came to Horeb,
the mountain of God. • *There the angel of Yahweh appeared to him in the*
shape of a flame of fire, coming from the middle of a bush. Moses looked;
there was the bush blazing but it was not being burnt up. • *'I must go and*
look at this strange sight,' Moses said 'and see why the bush is not burnt.'
• *Now Yahweh saw him go forward to look, and God called to him from*
the middle of the bush. 'Moses, Moses!' he said. 'Here I am' he answered. •
'Come no nearer' he said. 'Take off your shoes, for the place on which you
stand is holy ground. I am the God of your father,' he said 'the God of
Abraham, the God of Isaac and the God of Jacob.' At this Moses covered
his face, afraid to look at God.

Exodus 3:1–6

In this world the ordinary has always been the vehicle for
the extraordinary; in the midst of common routine the
totally 'other' suddenly breaks in. The material world in which
we live and the world of the spirit are not separate worlds but
one world of interwoven strands. Every so often we will become
suddenly aware of a greater depth of existence. Robert
Browning writes:

> Just when we are safest, there's a sunset touch,
> A fancy from a flower bell, someone's death,
> A chorus ending from Euripides –
> And that's enough for fifty hopes and fears

15

As old and as new at once as nature's self
To rap and knock and to enter in our soul.
                              (From 'Bishop Bloughram's Apology')

For Christians this is at its greatest in the incarnation of our Lord Jesus Christ, when the Word is made flesh and dwells among us (John 1:14). For those with their eyes open, the glory of God is ever being revealed in this world.

Moses was going about his normal business caring for the sheep of his father-in-law, Jethro, the priest of Midian. He was in the wilderness, a place of apparent emptiness. He was alert because he was keeping watch over his sheep. Suddenly he noticed a bush ablaze. Normally this would evoke only a little curiosity and perhaps cause the watcher to wonder who set it alight. But this bush was different – it burnt without being consumed. Moses was confronted with a mystery and out of the bush an angel of the Lord appeared. This great wonder caused him not only to turn from watching sheep but to turn back towards Egypt. Moses is discovered by God, rather than the other way round. In the receptivity of Moses God comes to him. Perhaps the emptiness of the desert was needed for this to happen. Moses does not call God, it is God who calls him. The initiative is God's and those whom he calls he sends. Though God initiates the action, it needs a human response. Moses would have to come to a decision. God promises that he will be with Moses from now on. Whatever you make of the burning bush there is no doubt that from then on Moses was aflame for God.

The revealing of the Holy One is what we need to transform our lives. We need to know that the ground on which we are standing is holy ground. When we have found one truly holy place then all places become holy. We need to be able to say with Jacob, 'Surely the Lord is in this place and I knew it not'. We may seek God, but we have to be open enough to let God find us. All our senses need to be alert to the God who comes.

16

> Earth is crammed with heaven
> and every common bush afire with God
> but only he who sees takes off his shoes
>> (Elizabeth Barret Browning, 'Aurora Leigh')

Think upon these words of de Chardin: 'God is not far away from us, altogether apart from the world we see, touch, hear, smell and taste about us. Rather he awaits us at every instant of our action.'

The desert is a great place for vision. Too often we are pre-occupied and God cannot enter our lives or our hearts; we have a label saying 'Full up'. As at Jesus' birth, there is no room in this establishment. We need to make space for the one who comes. We often see ourselves as seekers, but are we aware that God seeks us out, that he comes to us and reveals himself to us through his world?

> Holy God, make us holy.
> Revealing God, make us see:
> Open our eyes to your glory.
> Sending God, make us move,
> Open our ears to your calling.
> Loving God, make us love,
> Open our hearts to your love

6

God Calls

And Yahweh said, 'I have seen the miserable state of my people in Egypt. I have heard their appeal to be free of their slave-drivers. Yes, I am well aware of their sufferings. • I mean to deliver them out of the hands of the Egyptians and bring them up out of that land to a land rich and broad, a land where milk and honey flow, the home of the Canaanites, the Hittites, the Amorites, the Perizzites, the Hivites and the Jebusites. • And now the cry of the sons of Israel has come to me, and I have witnessed the way in which the Egyptians oppress them, so come, I send you to Pharaoh to bring the sons of Israel, my people, out of Egypt.'

Moses said to God, 'Who am I to go to Pharaoh and bring the sons of Israel out of Egypt?' • 'I shall be with you,' was the answer 'and this is the sign by which you shall know that it is I who have sent you ... After you have led the people out of Egypt, you are to offer worship to God on this mountain.'

Exodus 3:7–12

When God reveals himself he shows himself to be a God who cares, a God of compassion. Concerned with the poor and the oppressed, he seeks to help those who have no helper. God says, 'I have seen ... I have heard ... I am well aware of their suffering ... I mean to deliver them ... and bring them up out of that land ...' Any who become aware of the compassion of God must act in a compassionate way or move away from the vision they have seen. Vision demands response to its insights. To abuse another person or to neglect them is to show we have not assimilated what we say with our lips about the God of love. The compassionate one demands compassion; the God

18

of love demands that we love. The God who comes down to rescue demands that we come down also. One of my favourite descriptions of a priest is 'someone who has come down in the world'. We have to be found where the needs of our world are.

Over the sands of Holy Island someone is seen stuck in the tidal waters. They ring from an emergency safety telephone and tell of their suffering. Soon RAF Boulmer has a Sea King helicopter on its way. Sometimes the search light is on until they locate the person or persons. From the helicopter is lowered the winchman, who comes down to where the people are with the sole purpose of delivering them. One by one they are harnessed and raised to safety. They are lifted out of the danger that would engulf them and brought to safe and solid ground. In the same way our God sees, hears and comes to lift us up and deliver us. This is not a remote God but a God who cares and acts. This is the God who comes down to where we are.

We must delude ourselves into thinking we have a high position, or that we can easily cope with what lies before us. Many of the powers we have to face are alien and much stronger. In the case of Moses, he had already fled from the court of Pharaoh; he was now a nomadic shepherd being asked to pit his puny might against the power of the great Egyptian Empire. God needs someone to represent him. He often chooses the weak and the foolish so that through them his strength may be revealed. What he asks for is obedience: it is not whether we are able but whether we are willing that is important. In the Church of today there are great resources; if we came together we would be the richest organisation in the world in terms of human resources, but we often fail to answer the call through lack of volition. It is our unwillingness to react to the call that so often hinders God's work. God still calls us to dream of what could be. Like Martin Luther King we have to be able to say 'I have a dream'. In many ways the dream of Moses was like that expressed in the musical *The Man of La Mancha*.

To dream the impossible dream,
To fight the unbeatable foe,
To bear the unbearable sorrow,
To run where the brave dare not go,
To right the unrightable wrong,
To be better by far than you are,
To try when your arms are weary,
To reach the unreachable star
This is my quest . . .

(The Man of La Mancha, Joe Dann, 1965)

This is all suddenly earthed by the earth-loving God who says to Moses, 'I send you to Pharaoh'.

Loving God, you see our needs,
you hear our cry, you are aware of our sufferings,
you come down among us to lift us up.
Fill us with a zeal for justice and freedom:
send us out, in your power, to proclaim freedom and
peace for all peoples.

7

The Wholly Other

Then Moses said to God, 'I am to go, then, to the sons of Israel and say to them, "The God of your fathers has sent me to you". But if they ask me what his name is, what am I to tell them?' • And God said to Moses, 'I Am who I Am. This' he added 'is what you must say to the sons of Israel: "I Am has sent me to you".' • And God also said to Moses, 'You are to say to the sons of Israel: "Yahweh, the God of your fathers, the God of Abraham, the God of Isaac, and the God of Jacob, has sent me to you". This is my name for all time; by this name I shall be invoked for all generations to come.

'Go and gather the elders of Israel together and tell them, "Yahweh, the God of your fathers, has appeared to me, – the God of Abraham, of Isaac, and of Jacob; and he has said to me: I have visited you and seen all that the Egyptians are doing to you. • And so I have resolved to bring you up out of Egypt where you are oppressed, into the land of the Canaanites, the Hittites, the Amorites, the Perizzites, the Hivites and the Jebusites, to a land where milk and honey flow." • They will listen to your words, and with the elders of Israel you are to go to the king of Egypt and say to him, "Yahweh, the God of the Hebrews, has come to meet us. Give us leave, then, to make a three days' journey into the wilderness to offer sacrifice to Yahweh our God." • For myself, knowing that the king of Egypt will not let you go unless he is forced by a mighty hand, • I shall show my power and strike Egypt with all the wonders I am going to work there. After this he will let you go.

I will give this people such prestige in the eyes of the Egyptians that when you go, you will not go empty-handed. • Every woman will ask her neighbour and the woman who is staying in her house for silver ornaments and gold. With these you will adorn your sons and daughters; you will plunder the Egyptians.'

Exodus 3:13–22

We are always wanting to enclose God within the framework of our understanding; we would like to explain him and name him. In the attempt to put a name to God there is the desire to control him. God can no more be pressed between pages than we can a press and keep a living flower or person: words lose the 'mystery' and 'otherness'. We slowly learn that God is greater than all our thoughts and that the mind alone cannot contain him. The more we learn about God the deeper we come before the mystery of God and discover that we cannot begin to explain him.

Moses is discovering that it is more important to talk to God than to talk about him. Moses will be asked to convey his experience to others, so he asks of God, 'What shall I tell them about you? Whom shall I say that you are? What is your nature and name?' It was difficult for Moses to explain how he had been found by God, how God called him from the burning bush and how God had heard his people. Yahweh replies by linking his name with the verb 'to be'. God says, 'ehyeh asher ehyeh', which is usually translated, 'I Am who I Am.' In this sentence there might be a mild rebuke to the question of Moses, or an invitation to 'search me out and know me'. Many prefer the translation to be put into the future, so that it says, 'I will be what I will be.' No words or tense can do justice to the nature of God, what God is or what he will be. He will be revealed in what he has done, what he is and what he will be, within a living relationship with his people and creation. The wholly Other comes to us and is among us. The wholly Other can be discovered through a personal relationship that is described by the word 'faith': faith is more than a credal belief, it is a living relationship.

For Moses, the God of his fathers, the God of history, the God of past experience, the God who was, has become the living God with whom he has to do. The God who was recorded in story and proclaimed in preaching is the God that he now personally encounters. This is not the God he can relegate to the past, he is the living God who is present and active. God is the eternally present, the great 'I am'. This experience of Moses is something we all need to experience.

Moses receives his direction and authority from the present living God, the God who seeks a covenant relationship, who is to rescue and redeem his people. God does not say, 'I am almighty. I am good. I am peace giving'; he says, 'I am what I am'. God is not restricted by his attributes or by the way we recognise him. He is more than the sum total of all our experiences. He is the God who is the same yesterday, today and forever – the wholly Other with whom we have to do. God is not a static god but the God who is to be discovered actively involved in the newness of each day and each event. God cannot be contained in a predictable pattern; he will be met in new ways and in making all things new.

All that we do is within this great Other; nothing is outside of him or beyond him. Yet we may spend our lives seeking him who is present, or running away from him who seeks us out. He is the one and only God and he wants a living, vital relationship with us. It is a wonderful moment when God is able to enter our life and say 'I Am', when we discover he is not a theory but a personal God seeking a personal relationship.

> Holy and ever-living God,
> who was, and is, and is to come,
> make us aware of you:
> reveal to us your glory,
> encircle us with your love.
> May we know that you,
> who are beyond our comprehension,
> are in our hearts and lives;
> You, who are beyond our world,
> are yet within us and in all things.
> Holy God, make us holy,
> that we may ever dwell in you and you in us.

8

Man Stalls

Then Moses answered, 'What if they will not believe me or listen to my words and say to me, "Yahweh has not appeared to you"?' • Yahweh asked him, 'What is that in your hand?' 'A staff' Moses said. • 'Throw it on the ground' said Yahweh; so Moses threw his staff on the ground – it turned into a serpent and he drew back from it. • 'Put your hand out and catch it by the tail' Yahweh said to him. And he put out his hand and caught it, and in his hand the serpent turned into a staff . . . • 'so that they may believe that Yahweh, the God of their fathers, the God of Abraham, the God of Isaac, and the God of Jacob, has really appeared to you.'

Again Yahweh spoke to Moses, 'Put your hand into your bosom.' He put his hand into his bosom and when he drew it out, his hand was covered with leprosy, white as snow.

Exodus 4:1–7

M oses is probably the greatest leader of the Old Testament and one of the greatest leaders of all time but, like all of us, he is human and balks at the task. He expresses his reluctance in a way that many will do after him. God calls and calls and, given the chance, the human stalls. Moses is afraid of being rejected (4:1). He has been rejected by his own people once before and this is why he fled to the wilderness (2:11–14). One of the greatest reasons for not venturing is the fear of rejection. 'Perhaps the people will not accept me. Perhaps they will not like what I come to do.' Later we will hear of Christ himself being rejected: 'He came to his own and his own received him not.' Jesus warned his disciples that like him they would be scorned and rejected by men. To want to be forever

24

popular will hinder our willingness to take risks. If we only do what people wish, we will not help to change what is around us.

Moses was reluctant because he felt he was not suitable for the task ahead (3:11). Yet of all the Hebrews he had held a place in the royal court. He knew the way the court operated and he also had an air of authority. It is too easy to say, 'There must be someone more suitable. Here I am, Lord, look at me and send somebody else.' Very often we see a task that needs to be done and yet feel that somebody else should do it. We must take on responsibility for ourselves and for the vision that we have. When God calls us he also prepares us and empowers us to do what he would have us do.

'I would do it but I am not very good in public, I am not a good speaker.' Time and time again this is the escape route for many avoiding God's call. Moses complains of his own lack of eloquence (4:10; compare this with Jeremiah 1:6). God initially meets this objection by sending Moses' brother Aaron with him. Strange how he turned up at the right time!

There are many things that prevent us from going out in mission and Moses manages to find a good few of them: there is the feeling of unworthiness, the fear of the unknown, the reproaches and questions of the people, not to forget a host of other excuses. God will meet each of these excuses in turn and will conquer them with the divine promise, 'I will be with you'. Very often we allow our past to blind us to the present and the redeeming power of God at work in us both now and in the future. 'Who am I that you should choose me? There are more accomplished people, brighter people, stronger people, more vocal people: send someone else. The task is so great and I am so small.' All this is a wrestling not with our abilities but with our willingness and our trust in God. Today the Church has almost all the resources it needs; what it lacks is the willpower to get up and act. 'I am not sure I want to do it. Please, God, send somebody else.' God calls, man stalls. As ever, those who excuse themselves exclude themselves. (Read Luke 14:16–21.) There are always reasons for not doing things, but heed this warning:

> There is a tide in the affairs of men
> which taken at the flood leads on to fortune.
> Omitted, all the voyage of their life
> is bound in shallows and in miseries.

Too often today people are sidetracked into a game of trivial pursuits when they could be enjoying the adventure of life on the deep.

One of the tragedies of our times is the lack of a sense of vocation or purpose. People refuse to take on responsibilities. A long time ago I took to heart the words of the reformer John Bright who said, 'Join some great cause, you may not do much for it, but it will do a lot for you.' The burning bush was a visible sign not only of the presence but of the power and purpose of God. The Holy One seeks us out for obedience in that service which is perfect freedom. The question is far more about willingness than capability. Moses was to learn that God says, 'Go and I go with you' and to respond, 'Here am I. Send me'. Our responses show our faith.

> Lord, you do not call us to tasks that are beyond
> our energies,
> nor to stretch ourselves beyond our reach.
> Yet you call us to risk and to venture in your strength
> and your presence.
> Help us at all times to trust in you,
> and to give ourselves in your service and for your glory.

9

Going Backwards

After this, Moses and Aaron went to Pharaoh and said to him, 'This is what Yahweh, the God of Israel, has said, "Let my people go, so that they may keep a feast in the wilderness in honour of me,"' • 'Who is Yahweh,' Pharaoh replied 'that I should listen to him and let Israel go? I know nothing of Yahweh, and I will not let Israel go.' • 'The God of the Hebrews has come to meet us' they replied. 'Give us leave to make a three days' journey into the wilderness to offer sacrifice to Yahweh our God, or he will come down on us with a plague or with the sword.' • The king of Egypt said to them, 'Moses and Aaron, what do you mean by taking the people away from their work? Get back to your labouring.' And Pharaoh said, 'Now that these common folk have grown to such numbers, do you want to stop them labouring?'

That same day, Pharaoh gave this command to the people's slave-drivers and to the overseers. • 'Up to the present, you have provided these people with straw for brickmaking. Do so no longer; let them go and gather straw for themselves. All the same, you are to get from them the same number of bricks as before, not reducing it at all. They are lazy, and that is why their cry is, "Let us go and offer sacrifice to our God". • Make these men work harder than ever, so that they do not have time to stop and listen to glib speeches.'

The people's slave-drivers went out with the overseers to speak to the people. 'Pharaoh has given orders' they said: ' "I will not provide you with straw. • Go out and collect straw for yourselves wherever you can find it. But your output is not to be any less."' • So the people scattered all over the land of Egypt to gather stubble for making chopped straw. • The slave-drivers harassed them. 'Every day you must complete your daily quota,' they said 'just as you did when straw was provided for you.' • And the foremen who had been appointed for the sons of Israel by Pharaoh's slave-

drivers were flogged, and they were asked, 'Why have you not produced your
full amount of bricks as before, either yesterday or today?'

Exodus 5:1–14

Moses must have experienced a feeling of having been there before as he came before Pharaoh. Moses the man no longer looked like an Egyptian but more like a Bedouin. Yet there was something about him that gained him entry to the royal court. Moses might know God and what was God's will, but Pharaoh did not know the Lord. It was important for Pharaoh to establish that he was in control and that neither Moses nor his Lord could command him. Even here we see the beginning of a collision course not only between Pharaoh and Moses but between Pharaoh and God. To ignore the Creator of heaven and earth is full of dangers. Tyrants may seem in a position of great power but their day will come to an end, and God and his righteousness will prevail. In the move towards justice, God calls his people to act for him. Time and time again in the twentieth century the free world has been called upon to care for oppressed people. It is unfortunate to note that we often act only out of vested interests and not for freedom.

We should never underestimate the power of tyrants, they will not readily let go of anything that gives them power. It will be difficult in our time to reduce the debt of the Third World without some willingness on the part of those who hold power: banks and governments will need to show a new generosity and willingness to sacrifice. Shareholders and the electorate will all have to make sacrificial decisions. We could change the state of the poor nations but only if we are willing. So often it is not that we cannot, but that we will not: our hearts have become hardened.

Only too often when our grip on power is threatened the first weapon seems to be a tightening of the grip. Pharaoh took counter-measures against Moses and the Hebrews by keeping

them even more occupied. Like many leaders after him,
Pharaoh tried to prevent any rallies or meetings of people. His
remedy was to overwork them. To say that people are lazy is
still often a way of avoiding our responsibility. The Hebrews
were ordered to make the same quota of bricks but no straw
would be provided for them, they would have to seek their own
supplies. In a sense, this task of collecting straw may have
been what the poor people always had to do. For the Hebrews
it was literally the last straw, they were now convinced that
they could not continue under this oppression: something had
to be done. Like so many tyrants, Pharaoh turned the screw
once too often. Tyranny leads to anarchy.

Moses had come to bring his people to freedom, but at this
stage only succeeded in making their position worse. There are
very few soft options on the way to freedom. The plight of the
refugees from Kosovo in 1999 shows that dealing with a dic-
tator will initially cause pain to those whom we seek to help.
Evil will never relent of its spoils easily. In this world we are
often called to live in conflict with misused powers.

> God, as you call us to proclaim peace and gentleness,
> make us wise in our dealings,
> thoughtful in our actions, caring in our decisions,
> that we neither misuse the power given to us,
> nor oppress any people.

10

Why, Lord, Why?

The foremen for the sons of Israel went to Pharaoh and complained. 'Why do you treat your servants so?' they said. • *'No straw is provided for your servants and still the cry is, "Make bricks!" And now your servants have been flogged! . . .' 'You are lazy, lazy' he answered 'that is why you say, "Let us go and offer sacrifice to Yahweh".* • *Get back to your work at once. You shall not get any straw, but you must deliver the number of bricks due from you.'*

The foremen for the sons of Israel saw themselves in a very difficult position when told there was to be no reduction in the daily number of bricks. • *As they left Pharaoh's presence they met Moses and Aaron who were waiting for them. 'May Yahweh see your work and punish you as you deserve!' they said to them. 'You have made us hated by Pharaoh and his court; you have put a sword into their hand to kill us'.* • *Once more Moses turned to Yahweh. 'Lord,' he said to him 'why do you treat this people so harshly? Why did you send me here? Ever since I came to Pharaoh and spoke to him in your name, he has ill-treated this nation, and you have done nothing to deliver your people.' Then Yahweh said to Moses, 'You will see now how I shall punish Pharaoh. He will be forced to let them go; yes, he will be forced to send them out of his land.'*

Exodus 5:15–6:1

All suffering people seek a logical answer to their plight. We want to know the reasons and we will ask 'Why me?' The Hebrews are no different and want to know why there has been a sudden change in attitude on Pharaoh's part. Why had their life suddenly been made harder? No doubt there are many factors in the answer and most of them are not logical. The increased brutality of the Egyptians is a common reaction of many to ethnic minorities, as we have seen too often in the closing years of this century. The reasons given for such violence are nearly always poor ones; in this case the complaint is about the tally of bricks and the statement that the Hebrews are lazy. If it was not that it would be something else.

During this time of persecution of the Hebrew minority, their leaders are in a very difficult position. It is not surprising that the foremen seek to pass the blame on to Moses and Aaron. No doubt the words used were stronger than 'May Yahweh see your work and punish you as you deserve!' Moses the liberator is blamed for making their situation worse and giving the Egyptians an opportunity to slay them. So often, in history, the liberator is initially seen as making more trouble for the people he seeks to care for rather than easing their situation. Unless we are willing to risk this pain barrier in relationships and in our dealings with people, it is likely nothing will change and we will remain captive. It is not surprising that Moses feels let down and disillusioned: the people seem to be suffering more because of him and they are on the point of rejecting him. At this point it would be easy to lose faith. As the people have blamed Moses, we should not be surprised that Moses now turns to blame God. Each is implying in turn, 'You have got us into this mess'. The big questions begin with 'Why?' 'Why do you treat this people so harshly? Why did you send me here?' Many years ahead, when the Son of God is on the cross there will be the same cry, 'My God, my God, why?' On that day also there will seem to be no answer, the sky will turn black and the powers of evil will triumph – though only for a while, for God is in control and he cares for his people. In the case of the Christ he will rise out of the captivity of the grave, he will defeat the powers of the evil one and open for us the way to the Promised Land.

We discover that goodness is stronger than evil, for God is still in control. In the same way, love will triumph over hatred and in the end people will rejoice in the glorious freedom of the children of God. It is hard to be patient, it is hard to trust and obey, but we are all asked to do this in faith, to believe that God hears us, cares and will act. When we fear, when we are troubled, we need to hear the words of God: 'I am Yahweh.' 'You will see how I shall punish Pharaoh. He will be forced to let them go; yes, he will be forced to send them out of his land' (6:1). In the same way we will be rescued from the powers of the evil one and the grasp of death.

Lord our God, we give you thanks,
in the midst of life and its troubles you are
  there,
you know our needs before we ask,
you hear our cry before we utter it,
you are our God, caring and active,
you will bring us out of the captivity of sin
  and death,
you will free us from the tyranny of evil
and bring us to the fullness of life in your
  glorious kingdom:
through Jesus Christ our Lord, who lives and
  reigns with you and the Holy Spirit, now and forever.
Amen.

11

The God Who Comes

God spoke to Moses and said to him, 'I am Yahweh. • To Abraham and Isaac and Jacob I appeared as El Shaddai; I did not make myself known to them by my name Yahweh. • Also, I made my covenant with them to give them the land of Canaan, the land they lived in as strangers. • And I have heard the groaning of the sons of Israel, enslaved by the Egyptians, and have remembered my covenant. • Say this, then, to the sons of Israel, "I am Yahweh. I will free you of the burdens which the Egyptians lay on you. I will release you from slavery to them, and with my arm outstretched and my strokes of power I will deliver you. I will adopt you as my own people, and I will be your God. Then you shall know that it is I, Yahweh your God, who have freed you from the Egyptians' burdens. • Then I will bring you to the land I swore that I would give to Abraham, and Isaac, and Jacob, and will give it to you for your own; I, Yahweh, will do this!"' • Moses told this to the sons of Israel, but they would not listen to him, so crushed was their spirit and so cruel their slavery.

Yahweh then said to Moses, • 'Go to Pharaoh, king of Egypt, and tell him to let the sons of Israel leave his land'. • But Moses answered to Yahweh's face: 'Look,' said he 'since the sons of Israel have not listened to me, why should Pharaoh listen to me, a man slow of speech?' • Yahweh spoke to Moses and Aaron and ordered them both to go to Pharaoh, king of Egypt, and to bring the sons of Israel out of the land of Egypt.

Exodus 6:2–13

Here is a passage that is full of meaning and promise and we need to spend some time applying it to ourselves. Throughout the next few sections we will stay with these verses and look at them and their different facets. In Bible reading there should never be a desire to rush from chapter to chapter; when you come across a treasure or something of great beauty you should stay with it for a while.

Too often in our lives and in our prayers we imagine that our God is far away and that he has to be persuaded to hear us. Many people give the impression that prayer is a long-distance call and that our God is far, far way. But our God is a God who is ever near, as he was to Abraham, Isaac and Jacob – and he is near to each of us. God makes himself known to us if we open our lives and our wills to him. Revelation is not something that happened in the past and is now finished. God constantly reveals himself to us through his world and through his actions. Revelation is in itself something moving and living. God comes to us in various experiences: he comes as the Almighty, El Shaddai, as the Lord Yahweh, but he comes also in more concrete ways for he comes as the covenanting God who wants us to have a relationship with him. He comes as the God who hears our cry and responds to our distress; he comes to bring us freedom from our burdens and release from our slavery; he comes with an outstretched arm, and for us who are Christians this has a deeper meaning when we look at the Christ on the cross. This is a God who knows our plight and comes to us where we are. Our present situation may appear quite grim but our Lord has not forsaken us and seeks to bring us into greater freedom and fuller life: he comes as our deliverer.

None of this is to be forced upon us but the opportunity is given us. God says to us, 'I will adopt you as my own people and I will be your God.' Here is a great offer – we can become his people and let him be our God. How do we react? The sad comment about the Israelites is that they were too crushed in spirit to listen, and there is a danger that many people are already in a similar position today.

Take time to know that God comes to you to ease your burden and release you from captivity. God asks you to work for him.

Remember, God will not force himself upon you: it is up to you to open your life to him and allow him to change you. He is the God who hears and acts, the God who always comes to you. We talk of the advent of our God as if his coming was at some future date. Know that he comes today and he comes to you.

> Come, my Lord, and rule in my life.
> Come, most high one, come down among us.
> Come free us from our burdens.
> Come rescue us from our captivity.
> Come and send us out in your name.
> Come bring us into the glorious liberty of the
>   children of God.
> Come be our God and we shall be your people.

12

Release, Rescue, Redeem

And I have heard the groaning of the sons of Israel, enslaved by the Egyptians, and have remembered my covenant. • *Say this, then, to the sons of Israel, 'I am Yahweh. I will free you of the burdens, which the Egyptians lay on you. I will release you from slavery to them, and with my arm outstretched and my strokes of power I will deliver you.*

Exodus 6:5–6

I read about a film on the television: a man had been bitten by a rabid skunk and he was afraid that he would go mad, so he chained himself up in a barn. Once he had shackled himself and thrown away the key, he heard on the radio that a flood was on its way; it seemed that it would engulf the barn and he would be drowned. He did not want to be destroyed, just as he did not want to harm anyone else, but the situation looked hopeless. I didn't watch the film, it was hardly my idea of relaxation. But I recognised the story: the human had bitten something or been bitten by something, it endangers his well-being and makes him a danger to others. He becomes shackled, unable to do what he wants to do. It looks as if he will perish in this dangerous predicament, unless someone looks for him and rescues him. I am sure that in the film, unless he was utterly depraved, the man would be rescued. Somewhere out there was someone who loved him and cared enough to seek him and rescue him.

In the Bible we are shown a picture of humanity bitten by something that makes them quite mad. People turn away from good and do evil; they turn away from the living and loving God to a life that is limited and perishable. The Almighty offers help and the human refuses. But God continues to search and to care. The summary of this search is: 'God so loved . . . . that he gave his only begotten son that whosoever believes in him should not perish but have everlasting life' (John 3:16). However hopeless our situation, however heavy our burden, however strong our captivity, our God promises and is able to deliver. 'I will free you of the burdens . . . I will release you from slavery . . . with my arm outstretched and my strokes of power I will deliver you.'

Often I hear people talk of a saving God, a God of power and might, but more often I see them resisting his actions in their lives. Somehow what we say in our creeds is not allowed to enter our daily living. Our God has stretched out his arms for us; he has revealed his power and his love for us. How do we react to the saving power of God? All of us go through different stages in our lives; there are times of freedom and other times when we enter into captivity. Sometimes what started off as freedom becomes restrictive. It is all too easy for security to hold us too securely, or for possessions to possess us. Sometimes it is history that holds us in the sense that the decisions of the past will not let us move freely into the future. There is always the danger that we sell our freedom to avoid risk or to buy safety. At some stage in their lives most people find they have become trapped or imprisoned. We find the rescue of the Israelites exciting because it shows how our God cares and acts for all eternity.

We do not know how the Israelites descended into slavery. They had once been friends of the king but by their own fault, or by circumstance, there was a change of atmosphere. Work became hard labour, movement became restricted, life became a struggle. The Israelites could not do what they wanted to do, they had become slaves. God wants his people to be free, he is a God who liberates. God does not diminish our lives but seeks to extend them and enhance them: he created us for the glorious liberty of the children of God. To the captives of Israel, God sent the liberators Moses and Aaron with the message 'I will redeem you with an outstretched arm'. God is deeply concerned about the situation we are in. He waits with open arms to welcome us back into freedom: the father waits for his prodigal sons and daughters who are living impoverished lives to return to him and his love, and if we have become slaves he will buy us back.

In harder times every town had its pawn shop, a place where you could raise money by putting your watch or your wedding ring into hock: you didn't sell them but gave them as a surety for the money you had borrowed. The hope was that in better times you would redeem that which you had lost. It could be costly but it was always good when you redeemed what was yours. God says, 'I will redeem you; I will buy you back; I will pay whatever price is necessary to gain your freedom. I will do it with outstretched arms.' These last words could be looked upon as a prophecy, for the price of our freedom from the slavery of sin and death was Christ crucified.

> Lord, thine arms are stretching ever far and wide
> to enfold thy children to thy loving side.
> And I come, O Jesus: dare I turn away?
> No, thy love has conquered and I come today.
> Bringing all my burdens, sorrow, sin and care,
> At thy feet I lay them and I leave them there.
>
> (W. Walsham How, 1823–97)

13

The God Who Adopts

I will adopt you as my own people, and I will be your God. Then you shall know that it is I, Yahweh your God, who have freed you from the Egyptians' burdens.

Exodus 6:7

A nursing friend of mine said, 'People can stand a great deal of suffering when they have loving support, it is loneliness that is hard to bear. One of the worst feelings that can come to us is that no one cares, that we are unloved and unwanted.' In times of need – in fact, at all times – we need someone to turn to and to know that we are loved. It is amazing how much more we can achieve if we know we are loved and wanted.

The Hebrews moved from being friends of Pharaoh to being friends of no one. They were not accepted as free people any more, no one cared for them, they were subjected to slavery and rejection. The land they lived in was not their homeland and they were wanted only as cheap labour. So often this is the fate of ethnic minorities: they may be needed, they may be allowed to do the hard work, but rarely will they find themselves in positions of authority. It is amazing how friendless our world can be to some individuals or minority groups. The Hebrews were misused and abused; they could have landed up as one of the tribes that vanished forever from the face of the earth. We know they survived this persecution and many more that were to come. Here are a people with a resilience that has helped them to triumph. They are not easily defeated because they know they are loved by God, they know they are wanted. It is their faith that carries them through and this is expressed in the words 'I will adopt you as my own people, and I will be your God'.

When they were in need of care and protection God adopted them. They might be slaves and heavily burdened, they might be oppressed and hounded, but they were not alone and they were the children of God. They had a Father who cared for them, who heard their cries and came to their rescue. The Hebrews had done nothing to earn this, they were a small tribal group, they were poverty-stricken and lost. God in his great love took them up and gave them the power to be called children of God.

It is this same adoption that gives us the power to say 'Our Father' and in saying it to affirm that we are not left as orphans, not left without love; we are cared for and belong to him. One day we wake up and realise we have been in a far country of our own choice whilst our God had been waiting for our return with outstretched arms. We do not deserve this love, we could never earn it, but it is offered to us as God offers himself to us. The grace of God is that he gives himself to us and for us.

> Holy and Mighty One,
> Open our eyes to your presence,
> Open our hearts to your love.
> Help us to see we belong to you
> and to know you never cease to love us.
> Lord, you call us in our loneliness,
> You call us in our hunger,
> You call us in our emptiness,
> You call us back to you and your great love.
> Lord, this day we give ourselves, our whole being
> to you: through Jesus Christ our Lord.

14

I Will Be Your God

I will adopt you as my own people, and I will be your God. Then you shall know that it is I, Yahweh your God, who have freed you from the Egyptians' burdens.

Exodus 6:7

'I will be your God.' This is no static or one-way relationship. Love seeks a response: love needs a response. The Father has shown his love towards us. Will we respond? As God gives himself to us, we need to learn to give ourselves fully to him. It is only when we enter into this two-way relationship that we can experience the liberty that it brings, the new freedom and power. St Paul calls this 'the glorious liberty of the children of God.'

We want to say, 'Surely you have always been our God, from the very beginning of the world?' This is obviously true but God has not forced himself upon us nor have we ever fully understood the impact of this relationship. We have so often kept God at a distance. Somehow, we are able to distance the God who is nearer than breathing. We have ignored the presence and doubted the power. We have become blind to the mighty acts of God that happen every day of our lives. There has been a breakdown in our relationship and in our vision. We must tune what the Celts called 'the five-stringed harp', meaning our senses, until they vibrate again with the presence and glory of God. It is not that God does not act, it is we who have become dull. This renewal of relationships is a little like courtship: God will reveal himself to us more and more until our lives are full of his beauty and glory.

Like the Israelites we need to learn again that God travels with us and we travel with him. Remember that lovely quote in Acts: 'he is not far from any of us, since it is in him that we live, and move, and exist' (Acts 17:27). Learn to travel in God and rest in God. Far too often we have lost any sense of the presence. Obviously, the tougher the going the more we need to realise the power that is with us and yet not dependent on us. There is a great potential in our lives that lies unrealised and that potential is the power and presence of God. Until we discover this great treasure, we are like people dying of thirst whilst sitting on a great underground lake. It is amazing how we refuse to acknowledge the riches that are ours. Of course if he is to 'be our God' it means that we have to let God be God and to rule in our lives.

> Lord of all being, I give you my will,
> I give myself to you, all that I am, all I hope to be.
> I give you my hopes and my fears.
> I give you my whole being.
> For I am yours, I come from you, I belong to you.
> Let me know that you have created me.
> You give me life and power,
> You give me grace, your give me yourself.
> Lord, may I ever rejoice and grow in your love.

15

God Goes Before Us

'Then I will bring you to the land I swore that I would give to Abraham, and Isaac, and Jacob, and will give it to you for your own; I, Yahweh, will do this!'

Exodus 6:8

We are all pilgrims and we move forward to where no one has been before. We seek vision, we cannot see very far ahead, but we must move forward. We do not believe that this world is necessarily getting better but we also seek a kingdom that is not of this world, we are moving towards the Promised Land. It is right that we feel some restlessness for we have not yet arrived: here we have no abiding city. At all times we need to remember that our God has promised us he will bring us into possession of the Promised Land.

In this journey it is good to have guidance from other travellers throughout the ages: human experiences change little. We should not ignore the maps and signposts of the past, they are there for our safety and guidance. On Holy Island the Pilgrims' Way is marked out with posts to prevent pilgrims getting lost in the quicksands. The posts are aids to the journey but they are not the destination. We must make sure we have set our sights on our journey and not let ourselves be diverted from it. We talk of the Promised Land but we need to be sure our journey is into God and his love.

It is necessary to note that God himself leads us there. We will only arrive if we follow him: our obedience and God's promise are both necessary. Too many people look for the Promised Land but they do not want to follow the rules of that land. We need to remember that the kingdom can only come where his will is done. The kingdom comes in where and when the king is obeyed.

Towards the end of *The Pilgrim's Progress*, Mr Valiant for Truth has been explaining to Mr Greatheart how his parents had tried to put him off by telling him of the dangers and difficulties he would have to face. No doubt he would not have made it alone, but he was not alone: God went before him and with him. Then comes the song:

> Who would true valour see
> Let him come hither.
> One here will constant be
> Come wind, come weather.

We might be journeying into the great unknown but we are not alone. God promises to go before us. We may not know what lies ahead but we know who is there. He goes before us as an eastern shepherd goes before his sheep, leading us to better pastures and refreshing places. We are not left alone, we do not have to strive alone: our God is with us. Affirm throughout today:

Yahweh is my shepherd, I lack nothing . . .
Though I pass through a gloomy valley, I fear no harm;
beside me, your rod and staff are there, to hearten me.

(Psalm 23:1, 4)

> Lead us, heavenly Father,
> out of darkness into light.
> Lead from sadness to joy;
> from death to life eternal.
> Go before us in all that we do
> and give us your help and guidance.

16

Go and Tell Pharaoh

Yahweh then said to Moses, • *'Go to Pharaoh, king of Egypt, and tell him to let the sons of Israel leave his land'.*

Exodus 6:10–11

The test of many visions is the responsibility they bring. For Moses, it was good to hear God saying, 'I will free you of the burdens ... I will release you from slavery ... with my arm outstretched and my strokes of power I will deliver you. I will adopt you ... I will be your God ... I will bring you to the land ... and I will give it to you ... I, Yahweh, will do this!' (6:6–9). Many of us would delight in all this and it is good to meditate on for God promises us much the same. I love meditating on the peace that God gives and resting in that peace, but God then demands that I share that peace with others and that I seek to bring peace to all my relationships.

For Moses and the people of Israel, God promises a great future but it is dependent on obedience. If anything is to be achieved, Moses must face the situation as it is and seek to change it. God says to Moses, 'Go to Pharaoh, king of Egypt, and tell him to let the sons of Israel leave his land.' Seeking a gift and even guidance from God is one thing but obeying him is another. Often we want the gifts but not the commands, especially if the way ahead looks tough. So often in life it is not through our vision or our ability that we fail, but in our commitment and willingness. What God offers is wonderful, but once Moses realises that demands are to be made of him

45

he answers Yahweh to his face: 'Look,' said he, 'since the sons of Israel have not listened to me, why should Pharaoh listen to me, a man slow of speech?' Once again God calls and man stalls: if God's kingdom is to come his will must be done. God orders Moses and Aaron to go to Pharaoh. If they had not obeyed, the story of the Exodus would have ended there for the time being.

God is willing to work for us but he wants us to work with him. If we are willing to listen to God he will send us to speak against injustice and to oppose tyranny. Remember, without God we cannot, without us God will not. This is expressed in the words of St Teresa concerning Christ:

> Christ has no hands but your hands to do his work today,
> Christ has no feet but your feet to speed men on his way.
> Christ has no lips but your lips to tell men why he died.
> Christ has no love but your love to win men to his side.

There is no doubt that those to whom God reveals himself, he sends; as he calls us, he calls us to do his work in the world. In a world full of refugees, injustice, violence and evil, none of us can be without a challenge and a task to do. So often we wonder whether we should act, whether we should offer ourselves, and then fail to act. Jesus says, 'By their fruits you shall know them.' It will be by our actions we are judged rather than by fine words. It is no use being able to define justice if we cannot live by it.

> Lord, take my hands and let them work for you.
> Take my lips and let them speak for you.
> Take my heart and let it love for you.
> Take my will and let me work for you.
> At all times let me serve you, whom to serve is
>   perfect freedom.

17

God's Messengers

*On the day when Yahweh spoke to Moses in the land of Egypt, • he said
this to him, 'I am Yahweh. Tell Pharaoh, king of Egypt, all that I say to
you.' But Moses said to Yahweh's face, 'I am slow of speech, why should
Pharaoh listen to me?'*

*Yahweh said to Moses, 'See, I make you as a god for Pharaoh, and Aaron
your brother is to be your prophet. • You yourself must tell him all I
command you, and Aaron your brother will tell Pharaoh to let the sons of
Israel leave his land. • I myself will make Pharaoh's heart stubborn, and
perform many a sign and wonder in the land of Egypt. • Pharaoh will not
listen to you, and so I will lay my hand on Egypt and with strokes of power
lead out my armies, my people, the sons of Israel, from the land of Egypt.
• And all the Egyptians shall come to know that I am Yahweh when I
stretch out my hand against Egypt and bring out the sons of Israel from
their midst.' • Moses and Aaron obeyed; they did what Yahweh commanded them. • Moses was eighty years old, and Aaron eighty-three at
the time of their audience with Pharaoh.*

Exodus 6:28–7:7

It follows that those whom God sends become his messengers
and he gives them the power to do what he wants them to
do. At no stage of the journey will his messengers be on their
own: God and all his power will be with them. This passage is
very much a repeat of what was said in Exodus 4:15–16,
perhaps it is repeated here because we are about to enter a new
stage: we will see the mighty acts of God and the deliverance of
his people from captivity and death. God seeks people to bring
in his kingdom. If the world is to be changed, God seeks to

work through us and our dedication to him. To be a messenger of God means that you have spent time with him and sought to know his will.

Once obedience is offered it is possible for the mighty acts of God to take place. So often what prevents God is our God-given freedom; we reject what God wants us to do. It is through the obedience of Moses and Aaron that God will now work. It is worth looking at the age of the two leaders – Moses was said to be eighty and his brother eighty-three when they came before Pharaoh. Throughout history God chooses the weak and the foolish, the most unlikely, that his power may be revealed. Unless we bear this in mind, we could be forgiven for thinking that whatever their age these two men left it rather late in their lives to get going. They who were not that far from death would lead their people out of captivity and away from death towards the Promised Land. No age, no person is beyond the power of God and God can work through any who give themselves to him. It is never too late to give ourselves to our God. At a time when most people would be thinking of sitting back and being looked after, Moses and Aaron set out on the greatest adventure of their lives. We must learn not to give up for God does not give up on us.

The reason for sending Moses and Aaron is that 'all the Egyptians shall come to know that I am Yahweh, when I stretch out my hand against Egypt and bring out the sons of Israel from their midst'. God is to be seen in his mighty acts and this is still as true today as it was in the days of Moses. Moses is called to speak and act for God, he is to be God's instrument – so much so that Pharaoh will not be able to distinguish and will see Moses as God. In a way God is seen incarnate in Moses and in all his messengers. As the mouthpiece of God, Moses has to listen to God and say what he is told to say. This speaking for God is not just dependent on feelings – we all know that feelings can be liars – it is dependent on the relationship Moses has with God. We are told that Moses speaks to God as a man speaks with his friend, that they speak face to face. If we are ever to speak for God it can only be done after we have carefully and sensitively listened to him. Today there are too many people who want to talk *about* God before they have talked *to* him.

Moses and Aaron are called by God but it does not guarantee that they will be accepted by the Israelites or by Pharaoh. If Pharaoh will not heed God he will not listen to Moses and Aaron. The reverse is often true, if we will not listen to people it is very likely that we do not hear the word of God. Hearts, or ears, that are hardened to the cries of people will become hardened to God. Pharaoh is a good illustration of this, with his hardness of heart to the Israelites and to God.

> Lord, you call to us in the cry of the poor.
> You seek us in the needs of your people.
> You draw us in the demands of the dispossessed.
> Lord, make us aware of you in others and your
>   love for us at all times.

18

The Plagues of Egypt

*Then Yahweh said to Moses, 'Pharaoh is adamant. He refuses to let the
people go. • In the morning go to him as he makes his way to the water
and wait for him by the bank of the river. In your hand take the staff that
turned into a serpent. • Say to him, "Yahweh, the God of the Hebrews, has
sent me to say: Let my people go to offer me worship in the wilderness. Now,
so far you have not listened. • Here is Yahweh's message: That I am
Yahweh you shall learn by this: with the staff that is in my hand I will
strike the water of the river and it shall be changed into blood. • The fish
in the river will die, and the river will smell so foul that the Egyptians will
not want to drink the water of it." '*

*Yahweh said to Moses, 'Say this to Aaron, "Take your staff and stretch
out your hand over the waters of Egypt, over their rivers and their canals,
their marshland, and all their reservoirs, and let them turn to blood
throughout the land of Egypt, even down to the contents of every tub or
jar" '. • Moses and Aaron did as Yahweh commanded. He raised his staff
and in the sight of Pharaoh and his court he struck the waters of the
river, and all the water in the river changed to blood. • The fish in the river
died, and the river smelt so foul that the Egyptians found it impossible to
drink its water. Throughout the land of Egypt there was blood. • But the
magicians of Egypt used their witchcraft to do the same, so that Pharaoh's
heart was stubborn and, as Yahweh had foretold, he would not listen to
Moses and Aaron. • Pharaoh turned away and went back into his palace,
taking no notice even of this. • Meanwhile, all the Egyptians dug holes
along the banks of the river in search of drinking water; they found the
water of the river impossible to drink. • After Yahweh had struck the river,
seven days passed.*

*Then Yahweh said to Moses, 'Go to Pharaoh and say to him, "This is
Yahweh's message: Let my people go to offer me worship. • If you refuse to
let them go, know that I will plague the whole of your country with frogs.*

• *The river will swarm with them; they will make their way into your palace, into your bedroom, on to your bed, into the houses of your courtiers and of your subjects, into your ovens, into your kneading bowls.* • *The frogs will even climb all over you, over your courtiers, and over all your subjects." '*

Yahweh said to Moses, 'Say this to Aaron, "Stretch out your hand, with your staff, over the rivers, the canals, the marshland, and make frogs swarm all over the land of Egypt" '. • *So Aaron stretched out his hand over the waters of Egypt, and the frogs came up and covered the land of Egypt.* • *But the magicians did the same with their witchcraft, and made frogs swarm all over the land of Egypt.*

Pharaoh summoned Moses and Aaron, 'Entreat Yahweh' he said 'to rid me and my subjects of the frogs, and I promise to let the people go and offer sacrifice to Yahweh.' • *Moses answered Pharaoh, 'Take this chance to get the better of me! When I pray on your account and for your courtiers, and for your subjects, what time am I to fix for the frogs to leave you and your subjects and your houses, and stay in the river?'* • *'Tomorrow' Pharaoh said. 'It shall be as you say' answered Moses. 'By this you shall learn that Yahweh our God has no equal.* • *The frogs will go from you and your palaces, your courtiers and your subjects; they will stay in the river.'* • *When Moses and Aaron had gone from Pharaoh's presence, Moses pleaded with Yahweh about the frogs with which he had afflicted Pharaoh.* • *And Yahweh granted Moses' prayer: in house and courtyard and field the frogs died.* • *They piled them up in heaps and the land reeked of them.* • *But as soon as he saw that relief had been granted, Pharaoh became adamant again and, as Yahweh had foretold, he refused to listen to Moses and Aaron.*

Then Yahweh said to Moses, 'Say this to Aaron, "Stretch out your rod and strike the dust on the ground: throughout the land of Egypt it will turn into mosquitoes" '. • *Aaron stretched out his hand, with his staff, and struck the dust on the ground. The mosquitoes attacked men and beasts; throughout the land of Egypt the dust on the ground turned into mosquitoes.* • *The magicians with their witchcraft tried to produce mosquitoes and failed. The mosquitoes attacked men and beasts.* • *So the magicians said to Pharaoh, 'This is the finger of God'. But Pharaoh's heart was stubborn and, as Yahweh had foretold, he refused to listen to Moses and Aaron.*

Then Yahweh said to Moses, 'Get up early in the morning and wait for Pharaoh as he makes his way to the water. Say to him, "This is Yahweh's message: Let my people go to offer me worship. • *But if you do not let my people go, I shall send gadflies on you, on your courtiers and your palaces.*

The houses of the Egyptians will be infested with them, and even the very ground they stand on. But I shall set apart the land of Goshen, where my people live, on that day; there will be no gadflies there, and so you may know that I, Yahweh, am in the midst of the land. • I shall make a distinction between my people and yours. This sign shall take place tomorrow." ' • Yahweh did this, and great swarms of gadflies found their way into Pharaoh's palace, into the houses of his courtiers, and into all the land of Egypt, and ruined the country.

Pharaoh summoned Moses and Aaron. 'Go' he said 'and offer sacrifice to your God, but in this country!' • 'That would not be right' Moses answered. 'We sacrifice to Yahweh our God animals which Egyptians count it sacrilege to slaughter. If we offer in front of the Egyptians sacrifices that outrage them, will they not stone us? • We must make a three days' journey into the wilderness to offer sacrifice to Yahweh our God, as he has commanded us.' • Pharaoh replied, 'I will let you go to offer sacrifice to Yahweh your God in the wilderness, provided you do not go far. And intercede for me.' • 'The moment I leave you,' said Moses 'I will pray to Yahweh. Tomorrow morning the gadflies will leave Pharaoh and his courtiers and his subjects. Only, Pharaoh must not play false again, and refuse to let the people go to offer sacrifice to Yahweh.' • So Moses went out of Pharaoh's presence and prayed to Yahweh. • And Yahweh did as Moses asked; the gadflies left Pharaoh and his courtiers and his subjects; not one remained. • But Pharaoh was adamant this time too and did not let the people go.

Then Yahweh said to Moses, 'Go to Pharaoh and say to him, "This is the message of Yahweh, the God of the Hebrews: Let my people go to offer me worship. • If you refuse to let them go and detain them any longer, • you will find that the hand of Yahweh will fall on your livestock in the fields, horse and donkey and camel, herd and flock, with a deadly plague. • Yahweh will discriminate between the livestock of Israel and of Egypt: nothing shall die of all that belongs to the sons of Israel. • Yahweh has fixed the hour. Tomorrow, he has said, Yahweh will carry out this threat in all the land." • Next day Yahweh kept his word; all the Egyptians' livestock died, but none owned by the sons of Israel died. • Pharaoh had inquiries made, but it was true: none was dead of the livestock owned by the sons of Israel. But Pharaoh became adamant again and did not let the people go.

Yahweh said to Moses and Aaron, 'Take handfuls of soot from the kiln, and before the eyes of Pharaoh let Moses throw it in the air. • It shall spread like fine dust over the whole land of Egypt and bring out boils that

52

break into sores on man and beast all over the land of Egypt.' • So they took soot from the kiln and stood in front of Pharaoh, and Moses threw it in the air. And on man and beast it brought out boils breaking into sores. • And the magicians could not face Moses, because the magicians were covered with boils like all the other Egyptians. • But Yahweh made Pharaoh's heart stubborn and, as Yahweh had foretold, he refused to listen to them.

Then Yahweh said to Moses, 'Get up early in the morning and present yourself to Pharaoh. Say to him, "This is the message of Yahweh, the God of the Hebrews: Let my people go to offer me worship. • This time I mean to send all my plagues on you and your courtiers and your subjects so that you shall learn that there is no one like me in the whole world. • Had I stretched out my hand to strike you and your subjects with pestilence, you would have been swept from the earth. • But I have let you live for this: to make you see my power and to have my name published throughout all the earth. • High-handed with my people still, you will not let them go. • Tomorrow, therefore, at about this time, I will let fall so great a storm of hail as was never known in Egypt from the day of its foundation. • So now have your livestock, and everything that is yours in the fields put under cover: on man and beast, on all that remains in the fields and is not brought indoors, the hail will fall and they will die." ' • Some of Pharaoh's courtiers, terrified by Yahweh's threat, brought their slaves and livestock indoors, • but those who disregarded Yahweh's threat left their slaves and livestock in the fields.

Yahweh said to Moses, 'Stretch out your hand towards heaven so that hail may fall on the whole land of Egypt, on man and beast and all that grows in the fields in the land of Egypt'. • Moses stretched out his staff towards heaven, and Yahweh thundered and rained down hail. Lightning struck the earth. Yahweh rained down hail on the land of Egypt. • The hail fell, and lightning flashing in the midst of it, a greater storm of hail than had ever been known in Egypt since it first became a nation. • Throughout the land of Egypt the hail struck down everything in the fields, man and beast. It struck all the crops in the fields, and it shattered every tree in the fields. • Only in the land of Goshen where the Hebrews lived, was there no hail.

Pharaoh sent for Moses and Aaron. 'This time' he said 'I admit my fault. Yahweh is in the right; I and my subjects are in the wrong. • Entreat Yahweh to stop the thunder and the hail; I promise to let you go, and you shall stay here no longer.' • Moses answered him, 'The moment I leave the city I will stretch out my hands to Yahweh. The thunder will stop, and there will be no more hail, so that you may know that the earth belongs to Yahweh. • But as for you and your courtiers, I know very well that you have no fear yet of Yahweh our God.' • The flax and the barley were ruined, since the barley was in the ear and the flax budding. • The wheat and the spelt, being late crops, were not destroyed.

Moses left Pharaoh and went out of the city. He stretched out his hands to Yahweh and the thunder and the hail stopped and the rain no longer poured down on the earth. • When Pharaoh saw that rain and hail and thunder had stopped, he sinned yet again. • He became adamant, he and his courtiers. The heart of Pharaoh was stubborn and, as Yahweh had foretold through Moses, he did not let the sons of Israel go.

Then Yahweh said to Moses, 'Go to Pharaoh, for it is I who have made his heart and his courtiers stubborn, so that I could work these signs of mine among them; • so that you can tell your sons and your grandsons how I made fools of the Egyptians and what signs I performed among them, to let you know that I am Yahweh'. • So Moses and Aaron went to Pharaoh. They said to him, 'This is the message of Yahweh, the God of the Hebrews, "How much longer will you refuse to submit to me? Let my people go to offer me worship. • If you refuse to let my people go, then tomorrow I will send locusts over your country. • They shall cover the surface of the soil so thick that the soil will not be seen. They shall devour the remainder that is left to you, all that has survived from the hail; they shall devour all your trees growing in the fields; they shall fill your palaces, the houses of your courtiers, the houses of all the Egyptians. • Your forefathers and their ancestors will never have seen the like since first they lived in the country." ' Then Moses turned away and left Pharaoh's presence. • And Pharaoh's courtiers said to him, 'How much longer is this man to be the cause of our trouble? Let the people go to offer worship to Yahweh their God. Do you not understand that Egypt is now on the brink of ruin?'

So Moses and Aaron were brought back to Pharaoh. 'You may go' he said to them 'and offer worship to Yahweh your God. But who are to go?' • 'We shall take our young men and our old men' Moses answered. 'We shall take our sons and daughters, our flocks and our herds, because for us it is a feast of Yahweh.' • 'May Yahweh be with you if ever I let you and your little ones go!' Pharaoh retorted. 'It is plain you are up to no good. • Oh no! You men may go and offer worship to Yahweh, since that is what you wanted.' And with that they were dismissed from the presence of Pharaoh.

Then Yahweh said to Moses, 'Stretch out your hand over the land of Egypt to bring the locusts. Let them invade the land of Egypt and devour all its greenstuff, all that the hail has left.' • And over the land of Egypt Moses stretched his staff, and Yahweh brought up an east wind over the land and it blew all that day and night. By morning, the east wind had brought the locusts.

The locusts invaded the whole land of Egypt. On the whole territory of Egypt they fell, in numbers so great that such swarms had never been seen before, nor would be again. • They covered the surface of the soil till the ground was black with them. They devoured all the greenstuff in the land and all the fruit of the trees that the hail had left. No green was left on tree or plant in the fields throughout the land of Egypt.

Pharaoh sent urgently for Moses and Aaron. 'I have sinned against Yahweh your God,' he said 'and against yourselves. • Forgive my sin, I implore you, this once, and entreat Yahweh your God just to rid me of this deadly plague.' So Moses left Pharaoh's presence and interceded with Yahweh. • Then Yahweh made the wind veer till it blew so strongly from the west that it caught up the locusts and carried them off towards the Sea of Reeds. There was not one locust left in the whole land of Egypt. • But Yahweh made Pharaoh's heart stubborn, and he did not let the sons of Israel go.

Then Yahweh said to Moses, 'Stretch out your hand towards heaven, and let darkness, darkness so thick that it can be felt, cover the land of Egypt'. So Moses stretched out his hand towards heaven, and for three days there was deep darkness over the whole land of Egypt. • No one could see anyone else or move about for three days, but where the sons of Israel lived there was light for them.

Pharaoh summoned Moses. 'Go and offer worship to Yahweh,' he said 'but your flocks and herds must remain here. Your children may go with you too.' • Moses replied, 'But you must let us have means of offering sacrifices and holocausts to Yahweh our God. • Our livestock, too, must go with us; not one head of cattle must be left behind: it must be from our livestock that we provide for the worship of Yahweh our God; until we reach the place, we do not know ourselves what worship we shall have to offer Yahweh.'

But Yahweh made Pharaoh's heart stubborn, and he refused to let them

*go. Pharaoh said to Moses, 'Out of my sight! Take care! Never appear before
me again, for on the day you do, you die!' • Moses replied, 'You yourself
have said it: never again shall I appear before you.'*

Exodus 7:14–10:29

Once we could read of the plagues as if they were remote
from our world, now we pick up the daily paper and read
of polluted waters, melting ice caps, diminishing fish stocks,
unprecedented storms and global warming almost every day.
It would seem that the plagues could be upon us. It is useful
to look at the plagues of Egypt to see if there is anything for
us to learn. It could be suggested that the plagues came because
of the insensitivity of Pharaoh and his people.

There is no doubt that the year of the Exodus was a bad year
for Egypt. The first of the tragedies was that the waters became
tainted (7:14–18). As water is the very life source of the Egyptians and all peoples, this was serious indeed. For the
Egyptians the Nile was sacred, and had divine powers, so this
was an attack on their faith and their god. Plagues rarely come
singly, one follows another – we have seen this time and time
again in this century. Tainted water destroys fish and can drive
amphibians on to the land. For the Egyptians the frog was a
symbol of the life force, but here it is getting out of hand.
Instead of being life-renewing the frogs are now life-plaguing.
God can put this right but it is dependent on the willingness
of the people (8:1–15). Note how the dead frogs are gathered
into heaps, no wonder a plague of flies or gnats follows. Insects
that bite have always been a trouble along the banks of the
Nile, but this time they become completely out of hand
(8:16–32). Following on from the insects is the plague in cattle,
no doubt suffering from the bites (9:1–7). The boils on people
follow in the same fashion (9:8–12). Again, skin diseases and
disorders were endemic in the Nile area. In many ways it is
easy to see how one plague can follow another, perhaps in a

56

natural order: we must remember that God speaks and acts through his creation.

The hail storm was of a violent nature and very frightening as hail is virtually unknown in Egypt. It would seem that once one of the elements is upset the rest also are in disorder (9:13–35). It is interesting to read the practical advice on what to do in a hail storm. The locust plague, conversely, is a common event. These destroyers will eat all green life and so produce a famine wherever they go. By now Pharaoh's servants see Moses as the trouble and ask Pharaoh to be reasonable (10:1–20). The darkness for three days is also a common event; it happens when the air is filled with dust and is usually caused by a south-easterly wind in the early summer (10:21–29). Darkness, calamity, chaos – it would seem that evil is triumphing and their god is being defeated. In all the plagues there is a heightening of something that is not really unusual until it becomes a destructive force on a grand scale. Again, we have seen this more and more in the latter half of the twentieth century.

A verse to take seriously is 9:14, where all the plagues are threatened to be upon the heart (the phrase used in the Author-ised Version). There is a strange pattern of warnings that go unheeded, a telling of what will happen if they do not comply, a refusal to listen, then comes the plague, a plea for easement from their troubles, a backing off, and then a return to the old ways and a hardness of heart. If the heart is sick or people are stubborn, havoc will be caused. We can see many of our global troubles reflected in this pattern. In the western and northern world, for instance, we do not want to cut back on carbon dioxide emissions but we would like to prevent poorer countries from developing industrial capabilities. We even think of buying their rights from them so that we can continue to despoil the world. We must truly be suffering from a plague of the heart.

Lord, make our hearts your home.
Renew in us a sensitivity for creation.
Restore to us a gentleness towards your world.
Make us aware that all things are linked.
Help us to see we are all part of the same creation
and we are one in you, through Christ our Lord.

19

The Last Plague Is Death

Then Yahweh said to Moses, 'One disaster more I shall bring on Pharaoh and on Egypt, just one. After this he will let you go from here . . . Indeed he will drive you out! • *Instruct the people that every man is to ask his neighbour, every woman hers, for silver ornaments and gold.'* • *And Yahweh gave the people prestige in the eyes of the Egyptians, while Moses himself was a man of great importance in the land of Egypt, and of high prestige with Pharaoh's courtiers and with the people.*

Moses said, 'This is Yahweh's message, "Towards midnight I shall pass through Egypt. • *All the first-born in the land of Egypt shall die: from the first-born of Pharaoh, heir to his throne, to the first-born of the maidservant at the mill, and all the first-born of the cattle.* • *And throughout the land of Egypt there shall be such a wailing as never was heard before, nor will be again.* • *But against the sons of Israel, against man or beast, never a dog shall bark, so that you may know that Yahweh discriminates between Egypt and Israel.* • *Then all these courtiers of yours will come down to me and bow low before me and say: Go away, you and all the people who follow you! After this, I shall go." ' And, hot with anger, Moses left Pharaoh's presence.*

Then Yahweh said to Moses, 'Pharaoh will not listen to you; so that my wonders may be multiplied in the land of Egypt'. • *All these wonders Moses and Aaron worked in the presence of Pharaoh. But Yahweh made Pharaoh's heart stubborn, and he did not let the sons of Israel leave his country.*

Exodus 11:1–10

After all that has happened to the people of Egypt there is a threat of worse to come. Unless attitudes change, disaster looms; unless the heart is healed, death is for certain. It is

strange to discover at this point that the Israelites were actually on good terms with the Egyptians. That the Israelites were
able to borrow jewellery, gold and silver certainly suggests
friendly relations. It is also said that the manly form of Moses
was well liked among the servants of Pharaoh (11:3). Perhaps
the ordinary Egyptians also suffered at the hands of Pharaoh.

The last plague stands on its own and comes unannounced;
once it happens there is hardly any time for negotiation. God's
people know about it and are warned to prepare themselves so
that they are saved from destruction. The last plague is death,
and death brings about the release of God's people. In the
middle of the night, by the light of the full moon, the Israelites
go out with great speed. To stay, to stand still, is to risk death.
There is no way we can understand this plague or its selec-
tivity: this is as true of death today as it was in the time of
Moses.

Looking at all the things that are happening to our earth
and affecting our way of life, it seems that the majority are not
very concerned. Very few appear to mourn the loss of countless
species of creatures for ever; some even say, 'Does it matter?'
Does it matter that the land is polluted and much water
becomes undrinkable? Does it matter that sea life is decimated
and fish numbers are at an all-time low? Already many hearts
are hardened and people are saying, 'Whatever will be, will be.'
All of the plagues could be said to be common occurrences
magnified, and much the same is happening now all around
our world. By ignoring the results of our lifestyle we are mag-
nifying our troubles. Like Pharaoh, we put off taking action
and refuse to be moved by the events that speak so clearly to
us. Such insensitivity is already a sign of death.

But there is one plague we will not avoid whatever we do.
The last plague will affect us all one day and that plague is
death. Sometimes it comes suddenly, without warning, catching
us unprepared. Others get plenty of warning and can prepare –
or refuse to believe it is happening. For sure, it will come and

touch us and our loved ones. We hear that not even a dog will growl against God's elect for they will escape this trial without injury. It is good at this point to read Romans 8:31–39, and to rejoice in the fact that nothing can come between us and the love of God made visible in Christ Jesus – not even death.

This will be a time for symbols of protection, for affirming our belief in a God who hears, loves and cares, for rejoicing in the promise of the Passover that we are protected from death itself. We need to affirm: God so loves us that we shall not perish but have everlasting life.

> Blessed are you, Lord Jesus Christ,
> by your death you have destroyed death;
> by your rising to life you have opened for us
>   the way to glory.
> In you we rejoice that death is conquered,
> we are set free, for you have won the victory,
> Christ our Lord, who died and rose again, and
>   now live and reign with the Father and the Holy
>   Spirit, one God, world without end. Amen.

20

The Passover

*Yahweh said to Moses and Aaron in the land of Egypt, • 'This month is
to be the first of all the others for you, the first month of your year. Speak to
the whole community of Israel and say, "On the tenth day of this month
each man must take an animal from the flock, one for each family: one
animal for each household. • If the household is too small to eat the
animal, a man must join with his neighbour, the nearest to this house, as
the number of persons requires. You must take into account what each can
eat in deciding the number for the animal. • It must be an animal without
blemish, a male one year old; you may take it from either sheep or goats. •
You must keep it till the fourteenth day of the month when the whole
assembly of the community of Israel shall slaughter it between the two
evenings. • Some of the blood must then be taken and put on the two doorposts and the lintel of the houses where it is eaten. • That night, the flesh
is to be eaten, roasted over the fire; it must be eaten with unleavened bread
and bitter herbs. • Do not eat any of it raw or boiled, but roasted over the
fire, head, feet and entrails. • You must not leave any over till the morning:
whatever is left till morning you are to burn. You shall eat it like this: with
a girdle round your waist, sandals on your feet, a staff in your hand. You
shall eat it hastily: it is a passover in honour of Yahweh. • That night, I
will go through the land of Egypt and strike down all the first-born in the
land of Egypt, man and beast alike, and I shall deal out punishment to all
the gods of Egypt, I am Yahweh! • The blood shall serve to mark the houses
that you live in. When I see the blood I will pass over you and you shall
escape the destroying plague when I strike the land of Egypt. • This day
is to be a day of remembrance for you, and you must celebrate it as a feast
in Yahweh's honour. For all generations you are to declare it a day of
festival, for ever.*

*"For seven days you must eat unleavened bread. On the first day you are
to clean all leaven out of your houses, for anyone who eats leavened bread*

from the first to the seventh day shall be cut off from Israel. • *On the first day you are to hold a sacred gathering, and again on the seventh day. On those days no work is to be done; you are allowed only to prepare your food.* • *The feast of Unleavened Bread must be kept because it was on that same day I brought your armies out of the land of Egypt. Keep that day from age to age: it is an irrevocable ordinance.* • *In the first month, from the evening of the fourteenth day and until the evening of the twenty-first day, you are to eat unleavened bread. For seven days no leaven must be found in your houses, because anyone who eats leavened bread will be cut off from the community of Israel, whether he be stranger or native-born.* • *You must eat no leavened bread; wherever you live you must eat unleavened bread." '*

Moses summoned all the elders of Israel and said to them, 'Go and choose animals from the flock on behalf of your families, and kill the Passover victim. Then take a spray of hyssop, dip it in the blood that is in the basin, and with the blood from the basin touch the lintel and the two doorposts. Let none of you venture out of the house till morning. • *Then, when Yahweh goes through Egypt to strike it, and sees the blood on the lintel and on the two doorposts, he will pass over the door and not allow the destroyer to enter your homes and strike.* • *You must keep these rules as an ordinance for all time for you and your children.* • *When you enter the land that Yahweh is giving you, as he promised, you must keep to this ritual.* • *And when your children ask you, "What does this ritual mean?"* • *you will tell them, "It is the sacrifice of the Passover in honour of Yahweh who passed over the houses of the sons of Israel in Egypt and struck Egypt but spared our houses".' And the people bowed down and worshipped. The sons of Israel then departed, and they obeyed. They carried out the orders Yahweh had given to Moses and Aaron.*

Exodus 12:1–28

The Passover celebrates a new beginning, the birth or the rebirth of the nation, so it is given a new time as the start of the calendar. The calendar is to begin in the spring at the time of the departure of shepherds to 'green pastures'. For the Israelites the year will now begin in spring with the Passover moon and will be commemorated by the Passover offering: it will celebrate their being led out to the green pastures of the land flowing with milk and honey. The events that follow will give meaning to their lives and bring a new order to their year; these events will serve as a constant reminder of the power of God and their dedication to him. It is the time to celebrate that we have survived the darkness and deprivation and come into a fuller and richer life. This is not a one-off celebration but is to be for ever to rejoice in the saving acts of God.

The Passover celebrates a caring God who seeks to redeem, a God who is in control and sovereign over all. The Passover is to protect the Israelites from the destroyer who comes in the dark without warning. (12:13, 23, 27). It is a memorial to show that God delivers them from destruction and death, that God has made a covenant with them. The Passover is a time for community; it cannot be celebrated alone – at least ten males are needed plus, of course, their families. It is a time of common union, of communion with each other and with their God (12:1–3). As this is an offering to God, the best must be offered, it is not an excuse for getting rid of what we do not want or something not desirable or profitable to us – we have to give God of our best (12:5).

This is a special memorial and needs to be repeated every year. Every year they are to kill the Passover victim and make the sacrifice of the Passover; they are to keep the ritual (12:27). One of the reasons for the ritual is to educate the next generation, to remind the children of the mighty acts of God and how their ancestors obeyed God and carried out the orders Yahweh had given them. There is a great need to examine any ritual we have to see if it speaks to and challenges the generation we live in. Ritual must have meaning, even if it is simply the worship of God. Are we sure we have enough meaningful events that remind us of the love and the saving power of God? We need to make sure we have proper remembrances. There is a feeling that the nation that forgets God and all he has done will not prosper. Christians need to learn again how to celebrate the great saving acts of God. Our festivals and holy days need to have a high profile so that they can speak to us of the love and the abiding presence of our God. Likewise, we need to realise that the Holy Communion service is a celebration of the eternal offering of Christ of himself as our Passover lamb for our redemption and to bring us to eternal life.

> Lord, you have left us a wonderful memorial
> of your passion, death and glorious resurrection;
> a memorial of your presence, your power and
>   your love.
> Help us to be ever aware of these sacred mysteries
> and know in our lives the fruit of your redemption,
> rejoicing that you have triumphed over death, and
>   live and reign with the Father and the Holy
>   Spirit, one God, now and forever.

21

The Exodus

And at midnight Yahweh struck down all the first-born in the land of Egypt: the first-born of Pharaoh, heir to his throne, the first-born of the prisoner in his dungeon, and the first-born of all the cattle. • *Pharaoh and all his courtiers and all the Egyptians got up in the night, and there was a great cry in Egypt, for there was not a house without its dead.* • *And it was night when Pharaoh summoned Moses and Aaron. 'Get up,' he said 'you and the sons of Israel, and get away from my people. Go and offer worship to Yahweh as you have asked and, as you have asked, take your flocks and herds, and go. And also ask a blessing on me.'* • *The Egyptians urged the people to hurry up and leave the land because, they said, 'Otherwise we shall all be dead'.* • *So the people carried off their dough, still unleavened, on their shoulders, their kneading bowls wrapped in their cloaks.*

The sons of Israel did as Moses had told them and asked the Egyptians for silver ornaments and gold, and for clothing. • *Yahweh gave the people such prestige in the eyes of the Egyptians, that they gave them what they asked. So they plundered the Egyptians.*

The sons of Israel left Rameses for Succoth, about six hundred thousand on the march – all men – not counting their families. • *People of various sorts joined them in great numbers; there were flocks, too, and herds in immense droves.* • *They baked cakes with the dough which they had brought from Egypt, unleavened because the dough was not leavened; they had been driven out of Egypt, with no time for dallying, and had not provided themselves with food for the journey.* • *The time that the sons of Israel had spent in Egypt was four hundred and thirty years.* • *And on the very day the four hundred and thirty years ended, all the array of Yahweh left the land of Egypt.* • *The night, when Yahweh kept vigil to bring them out of the land of Egypt, must be kept as a vigil in honour of Yahweh for all their generations.*

Exodus 12:29–42

We have seen in our own time many an exodus of people out of captivity and oppression and into the unknown. The peoples of Kosovo, or the Kurds fleeing Iraq from the tyranny of Saddam Hussein and arriving in Turkey or Iran. We have seen the problems that a mass exodus brings and how the host nations cannot cope with the great numbers involved. We have seen great crowds walking with few possessions, if any, and not knowing where they are going – only that they have to leave where they are if they want to be free people. In every case it would have been easier if the oppression had eased to make the people willing to stay. Unfortunately oppressors tend to tighten their hold until people can take it no longer and suddenly in desperation there is a mass exodus. As always, the innocent suffer at the hands of tyrants. To win freedom is always costly and demands sacrifice.

Perhaps the number of deaths due to plague among the Egyptians was the spur for the Israelites to leave. In recent times we have been able to hear many 'great cries' of people who suffer, because the media is able to be there and record events. Death among the Egyptians and fear of death among themselves bonded the people in a new desire to escape to something better. Very often in our hearts we know there is something better if only we had the willpower and the courage to move. It is often at moments like this that a leader arises or a mass movement begins.

When we see pictures of ill-clad people trudging through snow-covered mountains, hauling young children and elderly along rocky paths, we see how desperate is their plight: they will risk anything to escape. Those who are afraid to face the mountains or enter the desert will remain in captivity: where there is no risk there will be no gain. We need to learn that anyone who is afraid of entering the desert will find it difficult to move towards the Promised Land. In all our lives things break down – old systems, old ideas, old relationships: often we are challenged to move forward, to risk the darkness. So often the desert, the darkness, is the place where we come to know and serve our God. The desert is not a place for us to settle in, but we must pass through it if we are to come to greater freedom and awareness. At the beginning of the ministry of Jesus it is interesting to find him alone in the desert and facing what lies ahead. For me the telling words concerning Jesus are 'the Spirit drove him out into the wilderness' (Mark 1:12). Movement is very often of God's making, and we talk of 'movements of the spirit'. Suddenly in our world new ways break in, from the coming down of the Berlin Wall to the moving of a whole race of people. So often what matters is that we have decided to move and have acted upon it.

The journey for the Israelites will be a long one: forty years is a lifetime. As long as we live, the exodus continues; this is as true for us as for those who left Egypt. We will fear for our own vulnerability and powerlessness, but let us rejoice that our Lord keeps vigil for us (12:42).

> Lord, you call us out to ways that we do not know,
> you ask us to risk and to venture for you,
> you are with us in the desert times, watching over us:
> at all times you are our strength and our shield.
> Help us to trust in your love and to be aware of your
>   power and protection.
> Let us know you go before us and seek to lead
>   us to the Promised Land.

22

Remembering Redemption

Yahweh spoke to Moses and said, • 'Consecrate all the first-born to me, the first issue of every womb, among the sons of Israel. Whether man or beast, this is mine.'

Moses said to the people, 'Keep this day in remembrance, the day you came out of Egypt, from the house of slavery, for it was by sheer power that Yahweh brought you out of it; no leavened bread must be eaten. • On this day, in the month of Abib, you are leaving Egypt. • And so, in this same month, when Yahweh brings you to the land of the Canaanites, the Hittites, the Amorites, the Hivites, the Jebusites, the land he swore to your fathers he would give you, a land where milk and honey flow, you are to hold this service. • For seven days you will eat unleavened bread, and on the seventh day there is to be a feast in honour of Yahweh. • During these seven days unleavened bread is to be eaten; no leavened bread must be seen among you, no leaven among you in all your territory. • And on that day you will explain to your son, "This is because of what Yahweh did for me when I came out of Egypt". • The rite will serve as a sign on your hand would serve, or a memento on your forehead, and in that way the law of Yahweh will be ever on your lips, for Yahweh brought you out of Egypt with a mighty hand. • You will observe this ordinance each year at its appointed time.

'When Yahweh brings you to the land of the Canaanites – as he swore to you and your fathers he would do – and gives it to you, • you are to make over to Yahweh all that first issues from the womb, and every first-born cast by your animals: these males belong to Yahweh. • But every first-born donkey you will redeem with an animal from your flocks. If you do not redeem it, you must break its neck. Of your sons, every first-born of men must be redeemed. • And when your son asks you in days to come, "What does this mean?" you will tell him, "By sheer power Yahweh brought us out of Egypt, out of the house of slavery. • When Pharaoh stubbornly refused to let us go, Yahweh killed all the first-born in the land of Egypt, of man

and of beast alike. For this I sacrifice to Yahweh every male that first issues
from the womb, and redeem every first-born of my sons." • The rite will
serve as a sign on your hand would serve, or a circlet on your forehead, for
Yahweh brought us out of Egypt with a mighty hand.'

Exodus 13:1–16

There are some special words in Chapter 13 that we need to take to heart: consecrate (v. 1), remembrance (v. 3), explain (v. 8), observe (v. 10). These words are not separate from each other but all part of a way of living, a guide to help us become the people that God wants us to be. We all need to have times of consecration, remembrance, explanation and observation in our lives. Without dedication and story in our lives we are poor indeed.

The consecration of the first-born is to recognise that all belongs to God, all living things, all creation. We belong to God and we should be dedicating our lives to him. God asks that we do what he would have us do so that we may become the people he would have us be. Little acts of consecration each day bind us to our God. I like to begin many a day with the words of St Patrick: 'I bind unto myself today the strong name of the Trinity; By invocation of the same, the Three in One and One in Three.' It is a good practice to consecrate ourselves, our loved ones and our home to our God every day.

Remember what God has done for you and for this world. Spend some time in remembering all the benefits that God has brought to you. Give thanks for the life, death and resurrection of our Lord: remember that 'he died for you'. God with a mighty hand brought you out of darkness and death into light and life eternal. Remember, this is without your effort: God's love and might has done all this for you. Think and thank. Again, this is part of all true worship. In many churches the height of this memorial is the Holy Communion service.

If you use any symbols or ritual they need to be self-explanatory or to provoke the question 'What does this mean?'. Often we talk about great mysteries but that should not be an excuse for mystifying people. Let us make sure that our actions speak as clearly as our words. I believe we all develop certain actions and rituals over time, so we need to check that what we do reveals what we think and say. If we do not talk about our faith to others, how will they learn? It is in explaining our faith that we help it to grow even more.

Observe certain events each year. There is good teaching value in keeping certain acts each year, just as we celebrate birthdays. The obvious events are Christmas, Good Friday, Easter and Pentecost, but others can also prove very enriching. Advent is a wonderful time to rejoice in the coming of God into our world and our lives. Lent is a time to risk the desert and seek to go forward in faith. Many a saint's day is good to enlighten us and Ascension Day ought always to uplift us. Observe the Church year and let it enrich you. Education is an important part of keeping any feast (vv. 8, 14), as is grateful remembrance.

> I give myself to you, Lord.
> I give my mind and its thinking.
> I give my memory and all remembering.
> I give my knowledge and all my learning.
> I give my will and my concentration.
> I give you all that I am, my heart and mind
>   and strength.
> I give you my whole being, knowing that you
>   ever give yourself to me:
> Through Jesus Christ our Lord

23

God in the Wilderness

When Pharaoh had let the people go, God did not let them take the road to the land of the Philistines, although that was the nearest way. God thought that the prospect of fighting would make the people lose heart and turn back to Egypt. • Instead, God led the people by the roundabout way of the wilderness to the Sea of Reeds. The sons of Israel went out from Egypt fully armed. • Moses took with him the bones of Joseph who had put the sons of Israel on solemn oath. 'It is sure that God will visit you,' he had said 'and when that day comes you must take my bones from here with you.'

From Succoth they moved on, and encamped at Etham, on the edge of the wilderness.

Yahweh went before them, by day in the form of a pillar of cloud to show them the way, and by night in the form of a pillar of fire to give them light: thus they could continue their march by day and by night. • The pillar of cloud never failed to go before the people during the day, nor the pillar of fire during the night.

Yahweh spoke to Moses and said, • 'Tell the sons of Israel to turn back and pitch camp in front of Pi-hahiroth, between Migdol and the sea, facing Baal-zephon. You are to pitch your camp opposite this place, beside the sea. • Pharaoh will think, "Look how these sons of Israel wander to and fro in the countryside; the wilderness has closed in on them". • Then I shall make Pharaoh's heart stubborn and he will set out in pursuit of them. But I shall win glory for myself at the expense of Pharaoh and all his army, and the Egyptians will learn that I am Yahweh.' And the Israelites did this.

When Pharaoh, king of Egypt, was told that the people had made their escape, he and his courtiers changed their minds about the people. 'What have we done,' they said 'allowing Israel to leave our service?' • So Pharaoh had his chariot harnessed and gathered his troops about him, • taking six hundred of the best chariots and all the other chariots in Egypt, each manned by a picked team. Yahweh made Pharaoh, king of Egypt, stubborn,

*and he gave chase to the sons of Israel as they made their triumphant
escape. • So the Egyptians gave chase and came up with them where they
lay encamped beside the sea – all the horses, the chariots of Pharaoh, his
horsemen, his army – near Pi-hahiroth, facing Baal-zephon.*

Exodus 13:17–14:9

When the Israelites left Egypt they did not take the obvious
trade route towards the land of the Philistines; if they
had gone by this populous route they would have met opposition all the way, including the Egyptian frontier guards.
Crowds of refugees are rarely welcomed in settled areas for
they disrupt ordinary life too much. If the Israelites faced
opposition from the start they would soon become disheartened
and want to return to the relative safety of Egypt. So instead
of making for the Mediterranean coast they went by the Sea
of Reeds.

The important thing to note is that God led them, guided
them, protected them. The Israelites were only beginning to
learn that wherever they went their God went with them. God
is there in the darkness and gives his light; he is there to
protect against the scorching heat of the day. God himself led
them and was to be known in the pillar of cloud by day and in
the pillar of fire giving them light at night. God was revealing
himself through his world and showing he is ever present. Do
we recognise the presence, the protection and the power of God
in our daily life?

In passing, there are two things of note: first, the Israelites
were armed and, secondly, they took the bones of Joseph with
them, as had been promised. The arms were not so much those
of an army but of individuals banding together to protect their
families and livestock. No group would think of travelling the
desert unarmed. Though they were a people in flight, they were
not totally disorganised. What they were now doing had been
planned for some time.

73

Their first day's journey was to Succoth; this was twenty-five miles, a hard trek for the young and the elderly, but they knew they had to set a distance between themselves and Pharaoh's army. There is always the fear of pursuit for refugees. It is perhaps for this reason that the Israelites altered their direction (14:1–4): they may have been trying to throw off any chance of being followed. However, a large group cannot move around a country without being noticed. It was brought to Pharaoh's notice that the Israelites were wandering to and fro in the wilderness. His courtiers persuaded him to seek the Israelites out and bring them back into slavery. So the Egyptians gave chase and came upon them near the Sea of Reeds.

As this is the story of redemption we must see what powers are at work. There are the powers of the world seeking to captivate and bring into slavery, and the power of God leading his people to freedom and the Promised Land. Do we put enough trust in the presence and power of God? Do we see God leading us in our daily activities? No doubt most of us need to spend time improving our vision.

> Give us, O Lord, a vision of your presence;
> help us to know you are near at hand,
> you are not far off and you are ready to
>   hear our prayer.
> May we become aware of your protection;
> May we know that you rescue us from darkness
> and guide us into the way of light and peace;
> For you are a loving and redeeming God,
> mighty in power.

24

Forward to Freedom

And as Pharaoh approached, the sons of Israel looked round – and there were the Egyptians in pursuit of them! The sons of Israel were terrified and cried out to Yahweh. • *To Moses they said, 'Were there no graves in Egypt that you must lead us out to die in the wilderness? What good have you done us, bringing us out of Egypt?* • *We spoke of this in Egypt, did we not? Leave us alone, we said, we would rather work for the Egyptians! Better to work for the Egyptians than die in the wilderness!'* • *Moses answered the people, 'Have no fear! Stand firm, and you will see what Yahweh will do to save you today: the Egyptians you see today, you will never see again.* • *Yahweh will do the fighting for you: you have only to keep still.'*

Yahweh said to Moses, 'Why do you cry to me so? Tell the sons of Israel to march on. • *For yourself, raise your staff and stretch out your hand over the sea and part it for the sons of Israel to walk through the sea on dry ground. I for my part will make the heart of the Egyptians so stubborn that they will follow them. So shall I win myself glory at the expense of Pharaoh, of all his army, his chariots, his horsemen.* • *And when I have won glory for myself, at the expense of Pharaoh and his chariots and his army, the Egyptians will learn that I am Yahweh.'*

Then the angel of god, who marched at the front of the army of Israel, changed station and moved to their rear. The pillar of cloud changed station from the front to the rear of them, and remained there. • *It came between the camp of the Egyptians and the camp of Israel. The cloud was dark, and the night passed without the armies drawing any closer the whole night long.* • *Moses stretched out his hand over the sea. Yahweh drove back the sea with a strong easterly wind all night, and he made dry land of the sea. The waters parted* • *and the sons of Israel went on dry ground right into the sea, walls of water to right and to left of them.* • *The Egyptians gave chase: after them they went, right into the sea, all Pharaoh's horses, his chariots, and his horsemen.* • *In the morning watch, Yahweh looked down on the army of the Egyptians from the pillar of fire and of cloud, and threw the army into confusion. • He so clogged their chariot wheels that they could scarcely make headway. 'Let us flee from the Israel-ites,' the Egyptians cried 'Yahweh is fighting for them against the Egyptians!' • Stretch out your hand over the sea,' Yahweh said to Moses 'that the waters may flow back on the Egyptians and their chariots and their horsemen.' Moses stretched out his hand over the sea and, as day broke, the sea returned to its bed. The fleeing Egyptians marched right into it, and Yahweh overthrew the Egyptians in the very middle of the sea. • The returning waters overwhelmed the chariots and the horsemen of Pharaoh's whole army, which had followed the Israelites into the sea; not a single one of them was left. • But the sons of Israel had marched through the sea on dry ground, walls of water to right and to left of them. • That day, Yahweh rescued Israel from the Egyptians, and Israel saw the Egyptians lying dead on the shore. • Israel witnessed the great act that Yahweh had performed against the Egyptians, and the people venerated Yahweh; they put their faith in Yahweh and in Moses, his servant.*

Exodus 14:10–31

The children of Israel have escaped from Egypt but their past is trying to catch up with them: behind them are Pharaoh and his army. The pull of the past is always strong and it enslaves many. We all tend to prefer security to the unknown: we choose safety rather than risk. Like many who have fled to freedom, the Israelites are suddenly faced with a trained army. We have seen this time and again in this century – poorly armed refugees facing up to tanks and guns. It is not surprising to hear that the Israelites are terrified and cry out to God. The other natural reaction is their anger towards Moses, he was their leader and responsible for getting them into this situation. He should have known what would happen. 'Were there no graves in Egypt that you must lead us out to die in the wilderness? What good have you done? . . . Better to work for the Egyptians than die in the wilderness!'

It is amazing how the pendulum swings: one moment you

76

are on the top of the world and the next you have plummeted to the depths: one day you are full of energy and life, the next you are drained out and cannot cope. One day life is full of food and flowers and the next we are in the wilderness. The desert is not just the Negeb or the Sahara, we can discover that the desert is within each of us. We are all capable of becoming a barren and dry land. In every life supplies can run low and we are no longer able to help ourselves. Suddenly we find ourselves between the devil and the deep blue sea.

At this point Moses says what seems almost impossible: 'Have no fear'. I am told that this phrase in its various forms can be found no less than 365 times in the scriptures. My favourite of the 'Do not be afraid' quotes is one I have already quoted – Isaiah 43:1–3. 'But now, thus says Yahweh, who created you, Jacob, who formed you, Israel: Do not be afraid, for I have redeemed you; I have called you by your name, you are mine. Should you pass through the sea, I will be with you, or through rivers, they will not swallow you up. Should you walk through fire, you will not be scorched and the flames will not burn you. For I am Yahweh, your God, the Holy One of Israel, your saviour.' How well these words fit the situation of the Israelites at the Sea of Reeds.

We need to learn to trust in the mighty God. Moses says, 'Stand firm, and you will see what Yahweh will do to save you today . . . Yahweh will do the fighting for you: you have only to keep still.' Too often we try to do what only God can do; we trust in our own ability and strength when we need to put our trust in the Almighty. Know that God is always at work on your behalf. To turn back is to die. We are called every day to reach out into the unknown with our trust in God. Moses is told, 'Tell the people to go forward' (14:15). These are some of my favourite words in the Book of Exodus and they come at a critical time. In front of the Israelites is a great expanse of water and swamp, and their fear of what might be. The people tremble on the edge of the Red Sea: the unknown threatens.

'We cannot go there, it has never been done before, it is not possible.' God says, 'Tell the people to go forward.' It is in the stretching of themselves, in the risking of security, in the reaching beyond reason, in the going where no one has gone before that they will discover the presence and the power of God. They will discover what Moses learnt at the burning bush. Moses said to God, 'Who am I that I should go?' And the Lord answered, 'I will be with you'.

'Tell the people to go forward.' It should never be forgotten that many opportunities and adventures are offered us. Too often it is not resources we lack but willpower; fear frequently expresses our lack of trust in God. By putting their trust in God and obeying his command, the Israelites are freed from their enemies and move towards the Promised Land.

> Guide me, O thou great Redeemer,
> Pilgrim through this barren land;
> I am weak, but thou art mighty;
> Hold me with thy powerful hand . . .
> Let the fiery cloudy pillar
> Lead me all my journey through:
> Strong deliverer,
> Be Thou still my strength and shield.
>
> (W. Williams, 1717–91)

25

Sing to the Lord

*It was then that Moses and the sons of Israel sang this song in honour of
Yahweh:*

*'Yahweh I sing: he has covered himself in glory,
horse and rider he has thrown into the sea.
Yah is my strength, my song,
he is my salvation.
This is my God, I praise him;
the God of my father, I extol him.
Yahweh is a warrior;
Yahweh is his name.
The chariots and the army of Pharaoh he has hurled into the sea;
the pick of his horsemen lie drowned in the Sea of Reeds.
The depths have closed over them;
they have sunk to the bottom like a stone.
Your right hand, Yahweh, shows majestic in power,
your right hand, Yahweh, shatters the enemy.
So great your splendour, you crush your foes;
you unleash your fury, and it devours them like stubble.
A blast from your nostrils and the waters piled high;
the waves stood upright like a dyke;
in the heart of the sea the deeps came together.
"I will give chase and overtake," the enemy said
"I shall share out the spoil, my soul will feast on it;
I shall draw my sword, my hand will destroy them."
One breath of yours you blew, and the sea closed over them;
they sank like lead in the terrible waters.
Who among the gods is your like, Yahweh?
Who is your like, majestic in holiness,
terrible in deeds of prowess, worker of wonders?*

You stretched your right hand out, the earth swallowed them!
By your grace you led the people you redeemed,
by your strength you guided them to your holy house.
Hearing of this, the peoples tremble;
pangs seize on the inhabitants of Philistia.
Edom's chieftains are now dismayed,
the princes of Moab fall to trembling,
Canaan's inhabitants are all unmanned.
On them fall terror and dread;
through the power of your arm they are still as stone
as your people pass, Yahweh,
as the people pass whom you purchased.
You will bring them and plant them on the
mountain that is your own,
the place you have made your dwelling, Yahweh,
the sanctuary, Yahweh, prepared by your own hands.
Yahweh will be king for ever and ever.'

Pharaoh's cavalry, both his chariots and horsemen, had indeed entered the sea, but Yahweh had made the waters of the sea flow back on them, yet the sons of Israel had marched on dry ground right through the sea.

Miriam, the prophetess, Aaron's sister, took up a timbrel, and all the women followed her with timbrels, dancing. • And Miriam led them in the refrain:

> *'Sing of Yahweh: he has covered himself in glory,*
> *horse and rider he has thrown into the sea'.*

Exodus 15:1–21

The whole of this song is probably an expansion of verses 20–21. As it was originally composed spontaneously it has a strength and natural feel to it. These are people who are celebrating their freedom on the other side of the Reed Sea; their God has gained them the victory. Because it sprang from the heart of the newly redeemed it does not bear cold analysis. There is a feeling of it being a popular song and destined to become part of liturgical praise. It would be used each year to celebrate God's victory and deliverance. Note also that this song is in the first person singular, it is meant for the individual to give their praise to God.

We need to build into our lives times and seasons when we give thanks for our creation, preservation and all the blessings of this life. We need to give thanks to our God that he has delivered us from captivity, from destruction and from death. Learn to rejoice in a redeeming God who rescues you from the powers of evil. Know that in the battle against evil and in the desire for freedom God is with you and on your side. Affirm that the Lord 'is my strength, my song, he is my salvation. This is my God, I will praise him' (15:2). Continue to affirm 'God is my warrior' (15:3). 'Your right hand, Yahweh, shows majestic in power . . . [and] shatters the enemy' (15:6). Seek to live knowing that God in his love for you seeks to protect you and to lead you. Sing to the Lord as his redeemed whom he leads by his strength and guides to his holy house (15:13), and he will be king for ever and ever (15:18).

At all times in this giving thanks for victory, be on your guard against making God your puppet, and speaking as if God were there to do your will rather than you to do his. There is often a danger of Christians being triumphal over any they feel are their enemies and suggesting 'God is on our side' and only ours. Commenting on this passage, Rabbi Johanan has said, 'When the Egyptians were drowning in the Red Sea, the angels in heaven were about to break into songs of jubilation. But the Holy One silenced them with the words "My creatures are perishing. Are you ready to sing?"' All suffering and all death should cause us sorrow. God loves us all. Christ has died for all, not only for a select few.

Let us compose a song of salvation to Christ our Lord. Let us sing of the conquering of death and the result that we are set free. Rejoice that, in his victory, Christ leads us out of darkness into his own marvellous light, out of hatred into love, out of despair into hope. Know that death has no more dominion over him and he will reign for ever and ever.

> Bless Yahweh, my soul,
> bless his holy name, all that is in me!
> Bless Yahweh, my soul,
> and remember all his kindnesses:
>
> in forgiving all your offences,
> in curing all your diseases,
> in redeeming your life from the Pit,
> in crowning you with love and tenderness,
> in filling your years with prosperity,
> in renewing your youth like an eagle's.

(Psalm 103:1–5)

26

Bitterness

Moses made Israel move from their camp at the Sea of Reeds, and they made for the wilderness of Shur where they travelled for three days without finding water. • They reached Marah but the water there was so bitter they could not drink it; this is why the place was named Marah. • The people grumbled at Moses. 'What are we to drink?' they said. • So Moses appealed to Yahweh, and Yahweh pointed out some wood to him; this Moses threw into the water, and the water was sweetened.

> *There it was he charged them with statute and with ordinance,*
> *there that he put them to the test.*

Then he said, • 'If you listen carefully to the voice of Yahweh your God and do what is right in his eyes, if you pay attention to his commandments and keep his statutes, I shall inflict on you none of the evils that I inflicted on the Egyptians, for it is I, Yahweh, who give you healing'.

So they came to Elim where twelve water-springs were, and seventy palm trees; and there they pitched their camp beside the water.

Exodus 15:22–27

In this life elation often gives way to depression, or simply the good times do not last and we have to be able to cope with harder times. The people who were redeemed (15:13), who sang in praise to the victorious God who does wonderful things, now descended into grumbling against Moses and against God. Although the murmuring is against Moses (v. 24) it inevitably involves a lack of trust and faith in their God. However, before we think we would do better it is wise to look at what caused their complaints.

The most essential thing for life after air is water. We can go without food for quite a long time but without liquid we soon perish. This is even more true in the desert where water is lost more quickly from the body. Travel in the desert had to be planned carefully for to run out of water meant death and before death there would be a period of all-consuming thirst. No doubt the time that Moses spent as a shepherd for his father-in-law, Jethro, taught him the way of the desert. Looking back he must have realised that God had been preparing him for this journey. Once Moses had led sheep through the desert, now he was being asked to shepherd the people of Israel. He had led them now for three days without coming to a watering place and people were beginning to feel distressed. As always the old and the young suffer first. Thirst was making people angry and fearful. At last they saw in the distance the watering place they were looking for and were relieved to see it. However, the water was so bitter they could not drink it (v. 23). The sour taste entered their spirits and they felt bitter against Moses. This was a bitter place and it made people the same. The people grumbled at Moses, 'What are we to drink?' (v. 24). This could have been the lowest point and it would have been easy for Moses to despair with them but he turned to the Lord. Surely the Lord who rescued them from Egypt and brought them through the Reed Sea did not bring them here to die in the wilderness. We are told that the Lord pointed out some wood to him and that when the wood was put in the water it made the water sweet and drinkable. There is no suggestion of a miracle here, though there is the suggestion that to those who trust in God all things work for the good.

We are reminded that 'Marah' means bitter (see Ruth 1:20). Very often in life people are disgruntled, they are not happy with their situation or with their leaders, and this bitterness is often expressed in complaints and murmuring. The Bible makes it clear that murmuring is dangerous for the communities and individuals who do it (see Exodus 14:10–12, 16:2–3,

17:1–2). Murmuring can soon destroy a person's or a community's well-being and some constant grumblers can keep a group of people continually disrupted and bitter. Let us be aware that much of our grumbling is directed towards God. In testing times grumbling usually only makes matters worse. God tested the people at Marah and promised that day, 'If you listen carefully to the voice of Yahweh your God and do what is right in his eyes, if you pay attention to his commandments and keep his statutes, I shall inflict on you none of the evils that I inflicted on the Egyptians, for it is I, Yahweh, who give you healing' (v. 26). God offers to protect and heal all who are obedient to him. As if to illustrate this the next oasis had a spring of water for each of the tribes of Israel and seventy palm trees (v. 27). Read Psalm 95.

> Lord, take away all bitterness and complaining
>   from our lives.
> Take away all grumbling about our community
>   and our neighbours.
> Help us to appreciate all that is done for us and
>   refresh our souls with your peace.

27

God Provides

From Elim they set out again, and the whole community of the sons of •
Israel reached the wilderness of Sin – between Elim and Sinai – on the
fifteenth day of the second month after they had left Egypt. • *And the whole*
community of the sons of Israel began to complain against Moses and Aaron
in the wilderness • *and said to them, 'Why did we not die at Yahweh's*
hand in the land of Egypt, when we were able to sit down to pans of meat
and could eat bread to our heart's content! As it is, you have brought us to
this wilderness to starve this whole company to death!'

Then Yahweh said to Moses, 'Now I will rain down bread for you from
the heavens. Each day the people are to go out and gather the day's portion;
I propose it to test them in this way to see whether they will follow my law
or not. • *On the sixth day, when they prepare what they have brought in,*
this will be twice as much as the daily gathering.'

Moses and Aaron said to the whole community of the sons of Israel, 'In
the evening you shall learn that it was Yahweh who brought you out of the
land of Egypt, • *and in the morning you shall see the glory of Yahweh, for*
he has heard your complaints against him – it is not against us you com-
plain, for what are we?' • *Moses said, 'In the evening Yahweh will give*
you meat to eat, in the morning bread to your heart's content, for Yahweh
has heard the complaints you made against him; your complaining is not
against us – for what are we? – but against Yahweh'.

Moses said to Aaron, 'To the whole community of the sons of Israel say
this, "Present yourselves before Yahweh, for he has heard your complaints" '.
• *As Aaron was speaking to the whole community of the sons of Israel,*
they turned towards the wilderness, and there was the glory of Yahweh
appearing in the form of a cloud. • *Then Yahweh spoke to Moses and said,*
• *'I have heard the complaints of the sons of Israel. Say this to them,*
"Between the two evenings you shall eat meat, and in the morning you shall
have bread to your heart's content. Then you will learn that I, Yahweh, am

your God."' • And so it came about: quails flew up in the evening, and they covered the camp; in the morning there was a coating of dew all round the camp. • When the coating of dew lifted, there on the surface of the desert was a thing delicate, powdery, as fine as hoarfrost on the ground. • When they saw this, the sons of Israel said to one another, 'What is that?' not knowing what it was. 'That' said Moses to them 'is the bread Yahweh gives you to eat. • This is Yahweh's command: Everyone must gather enough of it for his needs, one omer a head, according to the number of persons in your families. Each of you will gather for those who share his tent.'

The sons of Israel did this. They gathered it, some more, some less. • When they measured in an omer what they had gathered, the man who had gathered more had not too much, the man who had gathered less had not too little. Each found he had gathered what he needed.

Moses said to them, 'No one must keep any of it for tomorrow'. • But some would not listen to Moses and kept part of it for the following day, and it bred maggots and smelt foul; and Moses was angry with them. • Morning by morning they gathered it, each according to his needs. And when the sun grew hot, it dissolved.

Now on the sixth day they gathered twice the amount of food: two omers a head. All the leaders of the community came to tell Moses, • and he said to them, 'This is Yahweh's command: Tomorrow is a day of complete rest, a sabbath sacred to Yahweh. Bake what you want to bake, boil what you want to boil; put aside all that is left for tomorrow.' • So, as Moses ordered, they put it aside for the following day, and its smell was not foul nor were there maggots in it. 'Eat it today,' Moses said 'for today is a sabbath in honour of Yahweh; you will find none in the field today. • For six days you are to gather it, but on the seventh day – the sabbath – there will be none.' • On the seventh day some of the people went from the camp to gather it, but they found none. • Then Yahweh said to Moses, 'How much longer will you refuse to keep my commandments and my laws? • Listen! Yahweh has laid down the sabbath for you; for this he gives you two day's food on the sixth day; each of you is to stay where he is; on the seventh day no one is to leave his home.' • So on the seventh day the people abstained from all work.

The House of Israel named it 'manna'. It was like coriander seed; it was white and its taste was like that of wafers made with honey.

Moses said, 'This is Yahweh's command: Fill an omer with it, and let it be kept for your descendants, to let them see the food that I fed you with in the wilderness when I brought you out of the land of Egypt'. • *Moses said to Aaron, 'Take a jar and put in it a full omer of manna and place it before Yahweh, to be kept for your descendants'.* • *Accordingly, Aaron put a full omer of manna in the jar, as Yahweh had ordered Moses, and placed the manna before the Testimony, to be kept there.*

The sons of Israel ate manna for forty years, up to the time they reached inhabited country: they ate manna up to the time they reached the frontier of the land of Canaan. • *An omer is one-tenth of an ephah.*

Exodus 16:1–36

The travellers were refreshed and rested at Elim; it was like a little paradise in the desert. But they had not left Egypt to live in the desert, they were journeying to the Promised Land. No doubt the bitterness of Marah was forgotten for a while; they must have felt they were getting on well, that is until they entered the wilderness of Sin. The naming of this part of the desert has no link with our word 'sin', but is linked with the mountain of Sin that is called Sinai. By now the Israelites had been travelling for over a month and supplies were running low. At this stage there would be strict control of food through some form of rationing. Again people were feeling irritable, this time because they were hungry. Once more the grumbling begins, this time they idealised their past – a habit of us all – and thought of the abundance of food they had in Egypt (vv. 1–4). In their hunger they thought of 'food, glorious food', of cucumbers, melons, leeks, onions and garlic, as well as meat and fish (Numbers 11:4–5).

Then Yahweh, seeing their plight and hearing their groaning, provided for them (v. 4). The Lord seemed willing to put up endlessly with this moaning and groaning people, no doubt he knew they were ill-fitted for the desert. The Israelites were not left to their own resources which were running out: God sees, God cares and God acts. Though the people complained against

Moses, these complaints were in fact against God (v. 8). Despite all that they had experienced, the people still found it hard to trust in God. We must remember that as long as we live God has been with us, he has seen us this far and will see us further. Sometimes it is only when our resources run out that we realise that we have no power of our own to help ourselves and that our help comes only from the Lord. Those who have never run out of resources and believe themselves to be self-sufficient have not yet experienced the limits to which we can come. Only those who have exhausted their own resources truly understand the generosity of God and his redeeming love.

Quails migrate each year across the desert lands in the spring and again in the autumn. There is nothing unusual about a flock of weary birds dropping exhausted to the ground for rest, especially if the wind has been against them. I have seen birds coming from northern Europe drop with exhaustion on to the little island where I live, so tired that you could pick them up. The coming of the quails is not necessarily a miracle, but it depends how you look at life, for the timing is perfect. So often God meets our needs in the most natural of ways. Again, I am reminded of William Temple's saying: 'When I pray coincidences happen, when I do not pray coincidences do not happen.'

Manna can also be explained in a natural way. Today in the Sinai desert there is something that the Bedouin call 'mann'. This mann fits the description of manna in the Exodus: it is the honeydew excretion of an insect which lives in the tamarisk shrub. However, this mann can only be found in summer and it does not breed maggots, nor could it be found in great enough quantities to feed all of the Israelites. Too often we seek logical explanations when we are faced with mysteries. It is a pity that we seek answers for everything: life is a mystery to be enjoyed rather than a problem to be solved. In the rules about collecting the manna we see the need for faith, obedience and moderation – these qualities are signs of the people of God. It seems that God tests how well they show these qualities in their lives.

> O Lord, creator of all things, we put our trust
>> in you.
> In you we live and move and have our existence:
> without you we would become nothing.
> In times of weakness, when resources run low,
>> help us to trust in you,
> for you are our helper and our shield, a very
>> present help in trouble.

28

The Water of Life

The whole community of the sons of Israel moved from their camp in the desert of Zin at Yahweh's command, to travel the further stages; and they pitched camp at Rephidim where there was no water for the people to drink. • So they grumbled against Moses. 'Give us water to drink' they said. Moses answered them. 'Why do you grumble against me? Why do you put Yahweh to the test?' • But tormented by thirst, the people complained against Moses. 'Why did you bring us out of Egypt?' they said. 'Was it so that I should die of thirst, my children too, and my cattle?' • Moses appealed to Yahweh. 'How am I to deal with this people?' he said. 'A little more and they will stone me!' • Yahweh said to Moses, 'Take with you some of the elders of Israel and move on to the forefront of the people; take in your hand the staff with which you struck the river, and go. • I shall be standing before you there on the rock, at Horeb. You must strike the rock, and water will flow from it for the people to drink.' This is what Moses did, in the sight of the elders of Israel. • The place was named Massah and Meribah because of the grumbling of the sons of Israel and because they put Yahweh to the test by saying, 'Is Yahweh with us, or not?'

Exodus 17:1–7

Like the Israelites, we have to understand that the Lord knows our needs even before we ask of him. God knows that in this world we have basic needs that must be met. There are two contrasting dangers and, like the Israelites, we fall into both. The first is to lack trust in God. No matter what God has done for us in the past there is always the feeling he might not meet our genuine needs on this occasion. Even though God has provided in the past we wonder whether he can do so now.

91

It is amazing how unimpressed we are by evidence of God's love and power (see John 6:25–31). The other danger is to demand miracles, to forever desire special actions and to look only for the extra-ordinary.

At all times, every new situation challenges our abilities and our relationship with God. We must remember we are human, with human needs. The world we live in can be as dangerous as the desert and our supplies can suddenly run low. In the modern world we expect so much to be there for us in an instant: we are not used to having to look for water or going without water for very long. It is hard for us to understand how thirst will take over and fill our body and mind with longing. No amount of talking or grumbling will quench our thirst, only water will meet the need. No amount of study or religious acts will quench the thirst of the human soul, only God himself will meet that need.

Again, the grumbling against Moses is also against God (v. 3). There is a fear among them that children, cattle and they themselves will die and it is making them feel violent. Moses becomes afraid at their mood and turns to God, 'How am I to deal with this people?' he said. 'A little more and they will stone me!' (v. 4). God directs Moses to take some of the elders with him. It is a time to have the leaders of the people on his side as he acts out another of God's commands. They were to go to the forefront of the people. Moses was to take his staff with which he struck the river and go. It would be easy to ask, 'Go where?'. Moses trusted that God would be there before them. They may not know where they are going or what they are to do, but they do know who is there before them and who will meet them. Again here is an act of faith and obedience. Moses strikes the rock as he is commanded and water flows from it. Water from a rock is a possibility in the desert but the chances of finding the right rock must be millions to one. There may be a logical answer but in fact we are before a great mystery; the mystery is continuous in the survival of these people in the desert.

So often we create our own Massah and Meribah through our complaining about life and God. We also put God to the test by asking 'Is God with us or not?' (v. 7). Know that God is with you; if he were not you would not survive. Instead of being at Massah and Meribah, move to Bethel and learn to say, 'Surely the Lord is in this place'.

> O Lord, you are here,
> In my life, always with me
> And your presence is joy.
> You are here in the dark,
> In my life, always with me
> And your presence is light.
> You are here in my loneliness,
> In my life, always with me,
> And your presence is love.

29

Jethro's Visit

Jethro priest of Midian, father-in-law of Moses, heard of all that God had done for Moses and for Israel his people, and how Yahweh had brought Israel out of Egypt. • *So Jethro, father-in-law of Moses, brought Moses' wife Zipporah – after she had been dismissed –* • *with her two sons. One of these was named Gershom because, he had said, 'I am a stranger in a foreign land';* • *the name of the other was Eliezer because 'The God of my father is my help and has delivered me from the sword of Pharaoh.'* • *So Jethro, father-in-law of Moses, came with his son-in-law's wife and children to the wilderness where his camp was, at the mountain of God.* • *'Here is your father-in-law, Jethro, come to visit you,' Moses was told 'with your wife and her two sons.'* • *So Moses went out to meet his father-in-law and bowing low before him he kissed him; and when each had enquired of the other's health, they went into the tent.* • *Then Moses told his father-in-law all that Yahweh had done to Pharaoh and the Egyptians for the sake of Israel, and all the hardships that had overtaken them on the way, and how Yahweh had rescued them.* • *And Jethro rejoiced at all Yahweh's goodness to Israel in rescuing them from the Egyptians' hands.* • *'Blessed be Yahweh' said Jethro then 'who has rescued you from the Egyptians and from Pharaoh, and has rescued the people from the grasp of the Egyptians.* • *Now I know that Yahweh is greater than all the gods . . .'*

Then Jethro, father-in-law of Moses, offered a holocaust and sacrifices to God; and Aaron came with all the elders of Israel to share the meal with the father-in-law of Moses in the presence of God.

Exodus 18:1–12

Suddenly we get a glimpse of Moses as an ordinary human being with a wife and family as well as a father-in-law. No doubt news travelled across the desert of how Moses had escaped from Egypt and had defeated the Amalekites (17:8–16), or Moses may have even sent for his family. It may be that Jethro had information on where to find Moses or he may have sought out the area where he would expect him to be. It must have been exciting for this often lonely leader to hear that his family were riding towards them across the desert. Zipporah and the boys had probably been sent away for safety. Perhaps Moses feared for their well-being while he was negotiating with Pharaoh. A freedom fighter has often to sacrifice the comforts of his home for the cause, and of course there is the family sacrifice also in the separation from their loved one. The road to freedom is one that asks for sacrifices and it can be costly.

We are reminded of the names of the sons of Moses for they fit so well into the present situation. 'Gershom' was so-called because he said 'I am a stranger in a foreign land'. All his life Moses was moving on, a pilgrim towards the Promised Land. Ever since leaving Egypt for the first time Moses had the feeling of having no abiding city. It is good to put down roots or we may never grow but we also need to know that we have no abiding city. For us all, this world is a road rather than a resting place, we are all moving on and passing through. It is good to remember that the children of Israel never intended to live in the desert, they had their sights set on the Promised Land.

The name of the other son was Eliezer because 'the God of my father is my help and has delivered me'. Here is something very positive for us to affirm: 'God is my help and has delivered me.' This is a statement about our life and how we have come to this day; it is also a statement that gives us strength for the future. Without God we cannot achieve, but without us God will not achieve what he wills us to do. Moses relates to Jethro all that the Lord has done; this is Moses' testimony to the power of God in the lives of the Israelites. By the power of God this group of disorganised people became united and triumphed over the might of Egypt. God has led them by day and night, delivering them from hunger and thirst. There is no doubt that Yahweh is a mighty God; he is the Almighty God.

Sometimes it is suggested that Moses learnt of the worship of Yahweh from Jethro, and this may be so. This passage, however, seems to suggest the opposite. Jethro may have come to an awareness of Yahweh through the witness of Moses to the mighty acts of God. After listening to Moses, Jethro acknowledges that Yahweh is a redeeming and delivering God and greater than all gods (vv. 10–11).

We need to learn to witness to our God and to share what we have experienced with others. We need to tell what we have seen and heard and felt, to proclaim that our God is ever with us. Affirm these words:

> Though the dawn breaks cheerless on this isle today,
> my spirit walks in a path of light.
> For I know my greatness.
> Thou hast built me a throne within Thy heart.
> I dwell safely within the circle of Thy care.
> I cannot for a moment fall out of the everlasting arms.
> I am on my way to glory.
>
> (Alistair Maclean, *Hebridean Altars*, p. 55)

30

Sharing Leadership

On the following day, Moses took his seat to administer justice for the people, and from morning till evening they stood round him. • *Observing what labours he took on himself for the people's sake, the father-in-law of Moses said to him, 'Why do you take all this on yourself for the people? Why sit here alone with the people standing round you from morning till evening?'* • *Moses answered his father-in-law, 'Because the people come to me to bring their enquiries to God. When they have some dispute they come to me, and I settle the differences between the one and the other and instruct them in God's statutes and his decisions.'* • *'It is not right' the father-in-law of Moses said to him 'to take this on yourself.* • *You will tire yourself out, you and the people with you. The work is too heavy for you. You cannot do it alone.* • *Take my advice, and God will be with you. You ought to represent the people before God and bring their disputes to him.* • *Teach them the statutes and the decisions; show them the way they must follow and what their course must be.* • *But choose from the people at large some capable and God-fearing men, trustworthy and incorruptible, and appoint them as leaders of the people: leaders of thousands, hundreds, fifties, tens.* • *Let these be at the service of the people to administer justice at all times. They can refer all difficult questions to you, but all smaller questions they will decide for themselves, so making things easier for you and sharing the burden with you.* • *If you do this – and may God so command you – you will be able to stand the strain, and all these people will go home satisfied.'*

Moses took his father-in-law's advice and did as he said. • *Moses chose capable men from the ranks of the Israelites and set them over the people: leaders of thousands, hundreds, fifties, tens.* • *They were at the service of the people to administer justice at all times. They referred hard questions to Moses, and decided smaller questions by themselves.*

Then Moses allowed his father-in-law to go, and he made his way back to his own country.

Exodus 18:13–27

Jethro was able to watch Moses the 'judge' at work and was aware of how impossible the task had become. People were queuing all day to be interviewed by Moses so that he could dispense wisdom and judgement. Jethro could see the work wearied Moses and it was apparently endless. The people also became tired as they stood in the queue, which seemed not to move. Though Moses worked all day it was not enough (v. 13). Jethro took Moses to task at the end of the day and asked why he did it alone (v. 4). This is a question for all leaders, and the more gifted they are the more important the question. Ministry, caring for people, making judgements on behalf of the community – these always need to be shared. We need to see that we are all part of a team. The word 'team' can stand for 'to each a ministry'. Very often the churches that grow are those which allow people to exercise their share in ministry. Charismatic leaders are good and necessary but they must not be allowed to do what we should be doing for each other.

The reply of Moses to Jethro is a very noble one: Moses is acting for God and teaching the people about God's statutes and will (vv. 15–16). Obviously Moses felt an inner compulsion, and if he did not do it, who would? He was doing the work of God. Jethro was not to be swayed by this and told Moses, 'It is not right to take this on yourself. You will tire yourself out, you and the people with you. The work is too heavy for you. You cannot do it alone.' (vv. 17–18). Would that we all had a friend who could give us such sound advice. Too often leaders and individuals come to grief because of their own impossible ideals. It is good to have a friend who will help to earth our dreams and in doing so help to bring them to fruition.

Jethro, a wise old desert chieftain, gives wonderful advice to his son-in-law: 'learn to delegate'. Moses was advised to choose people of good moral standing, capable, God-fearing, trustworthy and incorruptible men, to look after groups and tribes according to their abilities (vv. 20–21). Moses was still to be in control, but only meeting the more difficult cases; the civic cases would be dealt with by the judges. Too often we do not heed good advice and then blame God when things go wrong. Take to heart Jethro's words to Moses: 'Take my advice, and God will be with you.' (v. 19). Read Acts 6:1–7 and Romans 12:3–13.

Do we take our part in ministry and do we encourage others to take their part? There is always the danger of thinking, 'Only I can do it. If I don't nobody else will.' We all have to stop one day and it is amazing how much of life will go on. In sharing, not only is life improved for all, but new talents are released. Too often we deprive potential leaders of the chance to contribute.

> Teach us, O Lord, to work as a team:
> Each of us offering ourselves,
> All our talents and abilities in your service.
> Make us to share in your ministry.
> Challenge our hearts with your love.
> Challenge our wills with your ways.
> Challenge our giving with your generosity.
> Challenge our minds with your mysteries.
> Challenge us to work together and to serve you.

31

On Eagle's Wings

Three months after they came out of the land of Egypt ... on that day the sons of Israel came to the wilderness of Sinai. • From Rephidim they set out again; and when they reached the wilderness of Sinai, there in the wilderness they pitched their camp; there facing the mountain Israel pitched camp.

Moses then went up to God, and Yahweh called to him from the mountain, saying, 'Say this to the House of Jacob, declare this to the sons of Israel, • "You yourselves have seen what I did with the Egyptians, how I carried you on eagle's wings and brought you to myself. • From this you know that now, if you obey my voice and hold fast to my covenant, you of all the nations shall be my very own for all the earth is mine. • I will count you a kingdom of priests, a consecrated nation." Those are the words you are to speak to the sons of Israel.' • So Moses went and summoned the elders of the people, putting before them all that Yahweh had bidden him. • Then all the people answered as one, 'All that Yahweh has said, we will do.' And Moses took the people's reply back to Yahweh.

Yahweh said to Moses, 'I am coming to you in a dense cloud so that the people may hear when I speak to you and may trust you always'. And Moses took the people's reply back to Yahweh.

Exodus 19:1–9

The Israelites had been travelling for three months, they had entered the wilderness of Sinai and now camped at the base of Mount Sinai. We have no sure idea of where this camp was or even which mountain was Sinai. The events that happened on the mountain far outweigh the importance of its whereabouts: the covenant with Israel was the important focus and the keeping of its conditions, rather than the site of a mountain top. It would seem that Sinai was not kept as a holy place. One of the simple reasons for this was that, as they moved to the Promised Land, Sinai was in a foreign country. God did not want a holy shrine, he wanted a holy people that obeyed him and did his will. The priority for us all is still to do the will of God. As the Israelites stayed in this area for a year there had to be enough pasturage for their livestock, enough water and provisions. Sinai was a necessary part of their journey, here they would consolidate their strength as a people, here they would set down ground rules for living and here they would make a covenant with their God.

The prelude to the covenant was a reminder of all that God had done for them – how he brought them out of Egypt and when necessary protected them. 'I carried you on eagle's wings and brought you to myself.' Often the scriptures refer to sheltering under the wings of God, but this is a different image. It was believed that when the right time came young eaglets were made to leave the nest. This was often done by cutting off their food supply and making their life uncomfortable for a while. The parent birds would soar above and encourage the young bird to take flight. Until then its home had been secure and on firm ground, now it was asked to take to the air. Surely it must be a strange moment when it launches out on its own. Suddenly it is caught in a cross-current and tumbles; it cannot cope on its own. Then the parent bird will fly underneath and support the falling bird. The eaglet will be encouraged to venture again and again, if necessary, until it can fly unaided.

God does this for his people, he does this for us, he bears us up when we fall. When we venture and risk and get into difficulties, he seeks to bear us up (see Deuteronomy 32:11). We can venture more than anyone else, for we know that underneath are the everlasting arms. God tells us what he has done and what he would like us to become. In this we are not alone for he is there to uplift us and support us (v. 4). We, like Israel, are his very own (v. 5) and he has called us to be a kingdom of priests and a consecrated nation (v. 6). When Moses tells the people of this call, they reply, 'We will do it.' Perhaps one of the reasons why we are not aware of the power and support of God is our unwillingness to do his will. God asks of us obedience and promises to care for us and uphold us.

It is good to learn to risk and adventure for God, knowing that at all times his hand is there to uphold us.

> O God, to turn away from you is to fall,
> to turn to you is to rise,
> to remain with you is to abide for ever.
> In all our duties grant us your help,
> in all our perplexities your guidance,
> in all our dangers your protection
> and in all our sorrows your peace;
> through Jesus Christ our Lord. Amen.
>
> (St Augustine of Hippo, 354–430)

32

Consecration

Yahweh said to Moses, 'Go to the people and tell them to prepare themselves
today and tomorrow. Let them wash their clothing and • hold themselves
in readiness for the third day, because on the third day Yahweh will descend
on the mountain of Sinai in the sight of all the people. • You will mark
out the limits of the mountain and say, "Take care not to go up the mountain
or to touch the foot of it. Whoever touches the mountain will be put to death.
No one must lay a hand on him: he must be stoned or shot down by arrow,
whether man or beast; he must not remain alive." When the ram's horn
sounds a long blast, they are to go up the mountain.'

So Moses came down from the mountain to the people and bade them
prepare themselves; and they washed their clothing. • Then he said to the
people, 'Be ready for the third day; do not go near any woman'.

Exodus 19:10–15

The prayer of Humble Access in the Holy Communion of the
Anglican Church begins: 'We do not presume to come to
this your table, O Lord, trusting in our own righteousness, but
in your manifold and great mercies.' Though God is loving and
caring we should not presume that we can come as we like
and do as we like. The Israelites were well aware that you
cannot come into the presence of a great person unprepared,
you can only come if they are willing and if you come with
due preparation. To come unprepared is to presume on God's
goodness and mercy; such an approach is in danger of ignoring
the holiness and the transcendence of our God. Those who lose
sight of the transcendence of God tend to lose the immanence
of God in trivialities and banal words.

103

Some of the early missionaries surprised the peoples of the Pacific Ocean by the way in which they so easily entered into the house of God. The so-called pagans called the Christians 'aholis', 'the people without breath'. Before they could enter their places of worship these islanders had to wait outside and prepare themselves properly. Sometimes, with our emphasis on the availability of God, we give the impression that people can come however they like. It would be far better for everyone if we taught them reverence and awe. We may need to learn again that 'Our God is a consuming fire'. The time before services in church is a good time to be silent and to prepare yourself to come before your God.

The Israelites are to prepare themselves for making their covenant with God: they are to get ready for his coming down to them. Later in history, when our Lord came down, the sad comment was: 'He came to his own domain and his own people did not accept him' (John 1:11). We need to take time to prepare ourselves for prayer or worship. We need a time of quiet dedication and consecration, when we set aside our normal activities to give ourselves fully to our God.

Covenants were often assumed by families or tribes, in a sort of gentleman's agreement. Likewise, a nation presupposed a covenant relationship with another nation. At other times the covenant had to be carefully worded and ratified. The more powerful of the two parties usually was able to dictate the terms. Moses went up to God to acclaim him as their victorious leader. God offered to lead them on his terms, as was common in suzerainty treaties. On the strength of what God had already done for them the people said they would accept his lordship: under his lordship they felt safe and secure.

If only we would reflect more often on what God has done for us. We spend so much time wanting more that we forget what we have already received. We need to remember the loving-kindness and mercy of our God. We have to learn that it is by grace we are saved and not by our own ability or goodness. Above all, we need to make space and time in our lives for God's coming to us. Note that it is not so much that the people come to God, it is that God comes down to them. This is at its fullest in the Incarnation of our Lord Jesus Christ.

> Almighty God, give us wisdom to perceive you,
> wisdom to understand you, diligence to seek you,
> patience to wait for you, eyes to behold you,
> a heart to meditate upon you and life to proclaim you,
> through the power of the Spirit of our lord Jesus Christ.
>
> (St Benedict, 480–543)

33

A Meeting Place

Now at daybreak on the third day there were peals of thunder on the mountain and lightning flashes, a dense cloud, and a loud trumpet blast, and inside the camp all the people trembled. • Then Moses led the people out of the camp to meet God; and they stood at the bottom of the mountain. • The mountain of Sinai was entirely wrapped in smoke, because Yahweh had descended on it in the form of fire. Like smoke from a furnace the smoke went up, and the whole mountain shook violently. • Louder and louder grew the sound of the trumpet. Moses spoke, and God answered him with peals of thunder. Yahweh came down on the mountain of Sinai, on the mountain top, and Yahweh called Moses to the top of the mountain; and Moses went up. • Yahweh said to Moses, 'Go down and warn the people not to pass beyond their bounds to come and look on Yahweh, or many of them will lose their lives. • The priests, the men who do approach Yahweh, even these must purify themselves, or Yahweh will break out against them.' • Moses answered Yahweh, 'The people cannot come up the mountain of Sinai because you warned us yourself when you said, "Mark out the limits of the mountain and declare it sacred" '. • 'Go down,' said Yahweh to him 'and come up again bringing Aaron with you. But do not allow the priests or the people to pass beyond their bounds to come up to Yahweh, or he will break out against them.' • So Moses went down to the people and spoke to them . . .

Exodus 19:16–25

I once arranged to meet a friend in front of a large hyper-market. Unfortunately it had three open sides to it and we waited at opposite ends of the building; somehow we missed each other even when we ventured to look around the building.

Later, we were able to communicate with each other and laugh at how we had failed to meet up. The next time we would make sure we were both going to be in the same place. There can be no lasting relationship with anyone, even our God, unless we have a meeting place. We must make sure we have a place where we have chosen to meet with our God.

The appearance of Yahweh on Mount Sinai is one of the most formative meetings in the whole of the Old Testament. Here God comes down to his people and talks directly to them. Like all arrivals of a special person, this appearance is preceded by a fanfare of trumpets to announce his presence: the nearer God comes, the louder the fanfare. Certain phenomena, which become lasting symbols of God, are also associated with this coming: there is the fire, the cloud and the deep darkness. The fire tells of the purity, the power and the unapproachability of God. The people are warned not to come too close: 'Take care not to go up the mountain or to touch the foot of it' (v. 12). There are limits which we cannot go beyond: our God is a transcendent God. In much of our modern teaching about the presence of God we are in danger of trivialising God and making that which is holy into something to be dispensed with ease. God is not a thing and is to be approached with awe and respect at all times. Only the consecrated, the holy, can approach in safety (Hebrews 10:10, 12:10; Romans 15:16; I Corinthians 6:19).

Because God is greater than the mind can conceive it is necessary to hide the fullness of his presence. No one can look upon God and live, so a cloud hides the fullness of his presence (19:9; cp. Deuteronomy 4:11, 12). In some strange way the closer we get to God the deeper the darkness we may experience (19:16–20). We know within ourselves that we need to be protected from the brightness and the glory. The cloud that hides the glory is one of the abiding symbols of Yahweh. Note how the mountain trembles at the presence. All things vibrate with his presence, all things tremble at the coming of God; can we alone stay unmoved (Hebrews 12:28)?

Time with Yahweh in the cloud has a twofold effect: it leads to the transfiguration of Moses (34:29–35) and the sending of him out in mission. 'Go down' said Yahweh to him, 'and come up again bringing Aaron with you.' Experience of the holy nearly always sends us out transformed and to bring others to that awareness. One of the tragedies of some missions is the sending out of people who have not spent time with the holy one. If we are to bring an awareness of God and his love to people we have to spend time with him and allow him to change us. We have to take time to be holy (Hebrews 12:4). While the people below were talking about God and building images, Moses was talking *to* God. We must make sure we talk to God rather than just about him and that our images do not prevent us from coming to him.

> I come before the Father, who created me.
> I come before the Son, who redeemed me.
> I come before the Spirit, who enlivens me.
> I come in love and adoration, to the One and
>   to the Three.
> I come in love and adoration, to the One and
>   to the Three.

34

The Commandments

Then God spoke all these words. He said, • *'I am Yahweh your God who brought you out of the land of Egypt, out of the house of slavery.*

'You shall have no gods except me.

'You shall not make yourself a carved image or any likeness of anything in heaven or on earth beneath or in the waters under the earth; • *you shall not bow down to them or serve them. For I, Yahweh your God, am a jealous God and I punish the father's fault in the sons, the grandsons, and the great-grandsons of those who hate me;* • *but I show kindness to thousands of those who love me and keep my commandments.*

'You shall not utter the name of Yahweh your God to misuse it for Yahweh will not leave unpunished the man who utters his name to misuse it.

'Remember the sabbath day and keep it holy. • *For six days you shall labour and do all your work,* • *but the seventh day is a sabbath for Yahweh your God. You shall do no work that day, neither you nor your son nor your daughter nor your servants, men or women, nor your animals nor the stranger who lives with you.* • *For in six days Yahweh made the heavens and the earth and the sea and all that these hold, but on the seventh day he rested; that is why Yahweh has blessed the sabbath day and made it sacred.*

'Honour your father and your mother so that you may have a long life in the land that Yahweh your God has given to you.

'You shall not kill.

'You shall not commit adultery.

'You shall not steal.

'You shall not bear false witness against your neighbour.

'You shall not covet your neighbour's house. You shall not covet your neighbour's wife, or his servant, man or woman, or his ox, or his donkey, or anything that is his.'

Exodus 20:1–17 (cf. Deuteronomy 5:6–21)

The time at the base of Sinai was an opportunity for the Israelites to explore who they were as a nation and what were their priorities: this was a time to for them to become a holy nation and to deepen their knowledge of God. The covenant relationship is based on what God has done and will do for them and what God requires of them to reflect his glory. In our terms, the 'ten words' (see Exodus 34:28 and Deuteronomy 4:13) are the basis of their relationship with God and with each other; they can be seen as the 'ground rules' for living. The 'ten words' are spoken directly by God to the people, though at other encounters Moses is the mediator between God and the people (20:19). God himself inscribed the words in stone – 'by the finger of God'. They are not to be seen as rules invented by Moses and they are not alterable.

If we are to be the people of God we are to seek to live by these standards. These ten words are the way God's people should act, and by this high code they will be known as his people. These words are to be the guidelines for all who want to serve him. They tell of our attitude to God, to each other and to the world. If God's rule, God's kingdom, is to come, it will come only through us and our willingness to say 'Your will be done'. These are not so much laws to follow as expressions of our love for God and his ways; our love for God is reflected in our relationships with each other. It even matters what we do in secret, for God sees in secret and he is there.

These 'commandments' are not case law originating out of past cases, though experience of the past always has a part to play: they are absolute and allow no exception. They are addressed to the individual. If your personal relationship with God is to be right you personally will live this way. This relationship is a result of God's redeeming love for us. Because God has won for us the victory, we are to give ourselves to him. He who frees us from slavery wants us to serve him in perfect freedom (v. 2). The whole of these 'commandments' must be

seen to be about grace rather than law; we keep this relationship with God and his creation because of what God does for
us.

We need to decide whether we will truly let God be God in
our lives. So much talk of God makes him sound as if he is our
servant and there to do our bidding when we want him. We
need to learn to adore and to give ourselves each day fully to
our God. If God does not have priority status in our lives, we
have not yet learnt of all he has done and continues to do for
us (v. 3). Nothing can depict or contain God fully. There is
always a danger of creating God in our image or according to
the latest trends in theology or philosophy, but in doing so we
limit him to our ability to see and reason – God is far greater
than we can see or know. Yet the God beyond reason is not out
of our reach or beyond our love. Beware of the danger of fixing
God in ways that suit what you want (v. 6).

The misuse of God's name is not just about blasphemy – that
is to make the words too small: it is about the misuse of God's
power. We should not use our God-given power in wrong ways:
this applies to the laws of nature as much as to the abilities
he has given to us. Profanity is always wrong but atomic
destruction is a greater misuse of God-given powers (v. 7). The
ways we use our resources reflect our attitude to creation and
its Creator.

This must be the first age that has sought to destroy the
sanctification of time. We now have machines that it is 'uneco-
omic' to rest and so we make people restless. We are in danger
of ignoring rhythms that are necessary to life, rhythms that
include stillness and rest. We also need to give time to God or
we will not get to know him (vv. 8–11). Busyness is in danger
of replacing godliness, even in some church communities.
Without a sabbath we justify ourselves by work rather than
grace and this is the plight of so many in our world.

How we react at home very often shows what we are really
made of, for here we are seen as we truly are. In all our

relationships, in our dealing with people, we reflect God's love or deny it (vv. 12–17). To be a holy people we must reflect God's holiness in our lives. No one can love God and not seek to obey him (John 14:15; 15:10).

Lord, we seek to serve you in love,
in the service which is perfect freedom.
We would obey your laws for there we show our love.
We would walk in your ways that we may walk with you.
We would seek to love others with the love you have for us.
Lord, let your laws guide us and your love enfold us,
that we may reveal your glory in our lives.

35

False Gods

When the people saw that Moses was a long time before coming down the mountain, they gathered round Aaron and said to him, 'Come, make us a god to go at the head of us; this Moses, the man who brought us up from Egypt, we do not know what has become of him'. • Aaron answered them, 'Take the gold rings out of the ears of your wives and your sons and daughters, and bring them to me'. • So they all took the gold rings from their ears and brought them to Aaron. • He took them from their hands and, in a mould, melted the metal down and cast an effigy of a calf. 'Here is your God, Israel,' they cried 'who brought you out of the land of Egypt!' • Observing this, Aaron built an altar before the effigy. 'Tomorrow' he said 'will be a feast in honour of Yahweh.'

And so, early the next day they offered holocausts and brought communion sacrifices; then all the people sat down to eat and drink, and afterwards got up to amuse themselves.

Exodus 32:1–6

One my favourite hates is waiting for someone who is late if I do not know why they are delayed. At Holy Island church I meet with many groups every summer and some come long distances. If a group is delayed I cannot guess what has become of them. Will they turn up at all? Has something happened to them? Waiting for the unknown gets hard to bear quite quickly. Obviously I need to pray for patience!

Think of the Israelites. Moses had gone up the mountain which trembled and smoked; he entered into the cloud and disappeared from their sight. They understand that it is a fearful thing to come too close to God (19:16–23). More than

113

five weeks have passed and he has not returned. The Israelites wonder what has happened to him: they have been left with a feeling of idleness and now a feeling of anxiety (v. 1). Moses left Aaron in charge, so, in their restlessness and nervousness, they turn to Aaron. They would like a more convenient god, a less dangerous god, a god who would do what they asked of him – or it. They need something to amuse themselves with. Moses has been the visible sign of God's presence, now they want something else in his place. They ask Aaron to make them a god (vv. 1, 4). Aaron could be manipulated more easily than Moses and did not take a firm stand. Now they could get rid of Moses and Aaron for a more accommodating way of life.

At their request Aaron had a bull calf made from their golden jewellery. Perhaps, for a moment, Aaron gambled on the hope that they would not give up their gold. It is said that Aaron cast the calf in a mould (v. 4) The Israelites feel that having a golden calf is permissible if they call it Yahweh. The bull was already a fertility symbol in the Middle East, and they were lowering Yahweh to the status of the Canaanite fertility gods. In our time we break commandments in the name of 'love' and say, 'It is allowable for God is the God of love.' This is not only taking God's name in vain, it is confusing our sexual urges with our deep longing for God. Too often in the name of God people are manipulated and misled. To mix our relationship with God with our desires and feelings is necessary but also a dangerous road. To give people only what they want is to end with a very low common denominator. We must aim for higher ideals and an adoring relationship with God. The religious groups that mix social revelry and ritual are walking a tightrope.

Aaron did not seem to mind making the calf. Later, he will blame the people for the calf and even blame the calf itself for being shaped the way it is (32:24). It is interesting how when we err we seek to apportion blame elsewhere: Adam blamed Eve and Eve blamed the serpent. Whilst Moses is meeting with

God the people are breaking the first three commandments (20:3–6). In modern terms, they have exchanged the reality of God for virtual reality, which is only fantasy. In the creating of idols and fixed images, we miss having a living relationship with God. No matter how good the image it cannot replace the true and living God. Anything less than God diminishes our freedom and our life. Though we are not worthy, God saves us and spares us through grace.

> I offer you my eyes and all my seeing.
> I offer you my ears and all my hearing.
> I offer you my mind and all its thinking.
> I offer you my heart and all its loving.
> I offer you my self and my full attention.
> I offer you my whole being, great God of life.

36

Breaking the Rules

*Then Yahweh spoke to Moses, 'Go down now, because your people whom
you brought out of Egypt have apostasised. • They have been quick to leave
the way I marked out for them; they have made themselves a calf of molten
metal and have worshipped it and offered it sacrifice. "Here is your God,
Israel," they have cried "who brought you up from the land of Egypt!" ' •
Yahweh said to Moses, 'I can see how headstrong these people are! • Leave
me, now, my wrath shall blaze out against them and devour them; of you,
however, I will make a great nation.'*

*But Moses pleaded with Yahweh his God. 'Yahweh,' he said 'why should
your wrath blaze out against this people of yours whom you brought out of
the land of Egypt with arm outstretched and mighty hand? • Why let the
Egyptians say, "Ah, it was in treachery that he brought them out, to do
them to death in the mountains and wipe them off the face of the earth"?
Leave your burning wrath; relent and do not bring this disaster on your
people. • Remember Abraham, Isaac and Jacob, your servants to whom by
your own self you swore and made this promise: I will make your offspring
as many as the stars of heaven, and all this land which I promised I will
give to your descendants, and it shall be their heritage for ever.' • So
Yahweh relented and did not bring on his people the disaster he had
threatened.*

*Moses made his way back down the mountain with the two tablets of the
Testimony in his hands, tablets inscribed on both sides, inscribed on
the front and on the back. • These tablets were the work of God, and the
writing on them was God's writing engraved on the tablets.*

*Joshua heard the noise of the people shouting. 'There is the sound of
battle in the camp', he told Moses. • Moses answered him:*

> *'No song of victory is this sound,
> no wailing for defeat this sound;
> it is the sound of chanting that I hear'*

As he approached the camp and saw the calf and the groups dancing, Moses' anger blazed. He threw down the tablets he was holding and broke them at the foot of the mountain. • *He seized the calf they had made and burned it, grinding it into powder which he scattered on the water; and he made the sons of Israel drink it.*

Exodus 32:7–20

God is in conversation with Moses and at the same time aware of what is happening in the base camp. God tells Moses what is going on. The people have rejected him, the 'jealous God', and so it follows that he rejects them. This is not what God wants but a relationship has to be two-sided. We cannot have the love of God in its fullness if we do not follow in his ways. Jesus says you cannot serve two masters; divided loyalty leads to endless difficulties. It is amazing how many people reject God, break his rules, and then assume they can have an easy relationship because of his love. As ever, those who excuse themselves from his presence, exclude themselves. God can say to them, because of their action, 'I never knew you.'

God is ready to destroy these idolaters and begin again through Moses. This could have been a test for Moses: does he care for these people with a deep love? Moses could become a second Abraham. Just as in the days of Noah when a new start was made, God could start afresh with Moses (v. 10). Moses shows his own depth as someone totally loyal to Yahweh and his glory. He is concerned for the fulfilment of God's work (v. 11), for God's honour in the eyes of the world (v. 12) and the sureness of God's covenant promises (v. 13). When God is described as relenting (v. 14) it does not mean a change of mind or position on God's behalf, it is a change in attitude made possible by altered circumstances, even if it is only Moses' pleading at this stage.

The Israelites did not deserve God's favour; they have put

God to the test. If God wanted to he could wipe them off the face of the earth. God could show his power, but instead he chooses to show his grace. God could lay down the law, instead he reveals his love. God, in love, has made a covenant with his people: he has promised to protect them and bring them to the Promised Land (23:20–33). We need to be aware of his grace, that he calls us out of love. He desires to bring us into his kingdom. At the same time, we must realise that if we are to be part of God's kingly rule, we must seek to do his will.

In the atmosphere high on the mountain, in the presence of Yahweh, Moses feels for the people. When he comes down from the mountain, he feels quite different. He is appalled by what he sees and hears. Ideals are shattered, the covenant relationship is being broken. In righteous anger Moses acts out what they have done and breaks the tablets of stone. It is a waste of time speaking to God on their behalf if they are going to ignore God. Moses feels strongly because he has the people in his heart and knows they are in the heart of God. We must not compromise God's character for ease or popularity. If people are going against the will of God, we should seek to direct them and set them aright.

There is nothing wrong with singing and dancing: they are wonderful gifts that God has given to us. More than once the scriptures enjoin us to sing and dance before the Lord, but here they are part of the diversion from God. We need to look at this seriously for we all invent diversions: we spend time on hobbies and watching 'soaps' on TV and then say we have little time if any for prayer and for developing our relationship with God. The rules are being broken every time we give something priority over God. Jesus said, 'Seek you first the kingdom of God.'

> Teach me, good Lord,
> to serve you as you deserve;
> to give and not to count the cost;

118

to fight and not to heed the wounds;
to toil and not to seek for rest;
to labour and not to ask for any reward;
save that of knowing that I do your will.

(Ignatius Loyola, 1491–1556)

37

Penitence and Promise

Yahweh said to Moses, 'Leave this place, with the people you brought out of
the land of Egypt, and go to the land that I swore to Abraham, Isaac and
Jacob I would give their descendants. • *I will send an angel in front of*
you; I will drive out the Canaanites, the Amorites, the Hittites, the Perizzites,
the Hivites, the Jebusites. • *Go on to the land where milk and honey flow.*
I shall not go with you myself – you are a headstrong people – or I might
exterminate you on the way.' • *On hearing these stern words the people*
went into mourning, and no one wore his ornaments.

Then Yahweh said to Moses, 'Say to the sons of Israel, "You are a head-
strong people. If I were to go with you, even for a moment only, I should
exterminate you. Take off your ornaments, then, that I may know how to
deal with you!"' So, from Mount Horeb onwards, the sons of Israel stripped
themselves of their ornaments.

Exodus 33:1–6

The result of Israel's sin is that they are asked to leave the
holy mountain. Sin separates us from God: sin and God
cannot be together, so sinners separate themselves from him.
Though they are separated from him by sin, God continues to
protect and guide his loved ones to the Promised Land. God
offers his guidance through a go-between in case he destroys
his people. Separation is not what God wills but what we do to
ourselves; though we leave him, he does not leave us. We will
end up either in adoration or destruction, and the choice is
ours. Though God is displeased it is for Israel's protection that
he acts, he still loves his people. Even when we forget God, he
does not forget us (33:3, 5; cp. Hebrews 12:29).

The description of Israel as 'headstrong' (v. 3) is a farming expression for an animal that refuses to be guided by the reins of its master. If an animal continues to be headstrong, no matter how much the owner loves it, he will have to cease to work with it. If we work against God and his ways, we cannot expect him to work with us. We need to understand who is God and who is in control. Much in the New Age is a desire to control and manipulate God. All who manipulate God, or think they do, are entering into the realms of magic. So often we go in the opposite direction to what God asks of us, and we wonder how it is we feel separated from him. I am reminded of the wayside pulpit poster which says, 'If you think that God is far away, who do you think has moved?'

As sin separates, repentance will set us on the road back. Jesus begins his message in St Mark with the words: 'The time has come and the kingdom of God is close at hand. Repent, and believe the Good News' (Mark 1:15). If we turn back we will discover that the Father has been waiting for us; he has not separated himself from us – we have turned away from him. God patiently awaits our return, and more than that he seeks out the lost as a shepherd would seek for a lost sheep (Luke 15).

When the Israelites hear of their new status they go into mourning for they have suffered a great loss indeed. Perhaps their not wearing jewellery was a sign of their misuse of it in making a false God. It is amazing how many Christians use the symbol of the cross like a talisman, when it is only God who can save.

> Lord, in the journey of life,
> when we stumble, raise us up;
> when we stray, redirect us;
> when we sin, forgive us;
> when we weaken, strengthen us;
> when we are weary, refresh us.

Give us all we need for the journey.
Take from us all that hinders us from
    coming to you
and bring us at the last to your glorious
    kingdom.

38

A Friendly Face

Moses used to take the Tent and pitch it outside the camp; at some distance from the camp. He called it the Tent of Meeting. Anyone who had to consult Yahweh would go out to the Tent of Meeting, outside the camp. • Whenever Moses went out to the Tent, all the people would rise. Every man would stand at the door of his tent and watch Moses until he reached the Tent; • the pillar of cloud would come down and station itself at the entrance to the Tent, and Yahweh would speak with Moses. • When they saw the pillar of cloud stationed at the entrance to the Tent, all the people would rise and bow low, each at the door of his tent. • Yahweh would speak with Moses face to face, as a man speaks with his friend. Then Moses would turn back to the camp, but the young man who was his servant, Joshua son of Nun, would not leave the Tent.

Exodus 33:7–11

A visitor to the church said, 'I do not want to take part, I just want to watch.' I wanted to say to the visitor, 'You cannot just watch, you are either part of what we are doing or you will not understand it.' Worship is not a spectator sport. Even if you sit at the back of a large church you are involved, or you are outside. Worship is about relationships and you cannot just watch. Though it often happens that by watching, people are drawn into the mystery and wonder and so led to take part in their own way. You either enjoy the presence of God or you ignore it; most of us do both at different times. It is good to affirm the presence of God every day. This does not make God come, rather it opens us up to his presence which is always there. Affirm today and every day:

You, Lord, are ... (you exist, you are Almighty, with us, etc.).

You, Lord, are in this place ... (where I am, where I am going, wherever I go).

You, Lord, fill this place ... (in you I live and move and have my being, I am in your heart, O God).

You fill this place with your love ... (peace, joy, hope, light).

In the beginning Moses was afraid and fearful of rejection, lacking in confidence, unsure of himself and his God. When Yahweh revealed himself at the burning bush, things began to change: the man who was full of excuses and unaware, gains confidence and walks in the awareness of the presence of God. Time and again, Moses had been totally dependent on the power and the grace of God. Yahweh had given the Israelites victory over the Egyptians and over the desert. God was truly his friend. With God as your friend, you cannot help but be confident. Abraham Lincoln declared, 'God plus one is a majority.'

The Tent of Meeting was placed outside the camp because it reflected the holiness of God as against the sinfulness of the people. To meet with Yahweh, the people would go outside the camp to this holy meeting place; in so doing they witnessed to their need of their God. It is important that our holy places are not made too common. Though God is present with us and within us, if we do not have some special meeting place it will be likely that we tend to forget his presence and ignore his demands. Create a holy place, a special part of your room or your garden, for times of quiet and conversation with God. Keep your holy place as somewhere special. For most people, all places can only be seen as holy once they have discovered one holy place. For this reason special holy places like Lindisfarne are important in our search for God, who is ever with us.

At the Tent of Meeting, Moses enjoys a special relationship with God that would seem to have no equal in all of the Old Testament. At the beginning of his call Moses was unsure about the nature of Yahweh who appeared before him at the burning bush; he was also lacking in confidence about his own ability and powers. Through the desert experience, Moses learnt of the love and care of the Almighty. Time and again he has relied on the goodness and grace of God, now he is known as a friend of God. There is a suggestion that Moses and God met up regularly and had a deep and meaningful relationship (vv. 9, 11).

The people watched with reverence and awe the signs of these encounters but they did not come to the Tent of Meeting. It is a great pity they stood afar off, for God wants us all to know his nearness. We cannot be just observers: worship is like love, you cannot be an onlooker, you have to be involved and committed to know what it is about. We have to seek our own personal awareness of the love of God; being told is not enough, we need to know for ourselves. 'Yahweh would speak with Moses face to face, as a man speaks with his friend.' (v. 11). Joshua, the son of Nun, learns from Moses and abides in the presence of God. We need to create our own Tent of Meeting, and to practise being in the presence of God.

> O great and glorious God,
> grant me a glimpse of your presence:
> make me aware of your love.
> May I know that I live in you,
> and that you are ever with me.
> You are my rock, my strength.
> You are my joy and my hope.
> You, dear Lord, are my everlasting Friend.
> May I rejoice in your love for ever.

39

My Presence Will Go with You

Moses said to Yahweh, 'See, you yourself say to me, "Make the people go on", but you do not let me know who it is you will send with me. Yet you yourself have said, "I know you by name and you have won my favour". •
If indeed I have won your favour, please show me your ways, so that I can understand you and win your favour. Remember, too, that this nation is your own people.' Yahweh replied, 'I myself will go with you, and I will give you rest'. • *Moses said, 'If you are not going with us yourself, do not make us leave this place. By what means can it be known that I, I and my people, have won your favour, if not by your going with us? By this we shall be marked out, I and my people, from all the peoples on the face of the earth.'* • *Yahweh said to Moses, 'Again I will do what you have asked, because you have won my favour and because I know you by name'.*

Exodus 33:12–17

Moving is often difficult for us as it means going into the unknown. To go forward means risking our security and comfort, sometimes risking our lives. Moses has been told it is time for the Israelites to move; they have been near to Mount Sinai for a year and some are obviously getting settled. God asks Moses to go forward to the Promised Land (33:1). If the people are to become what God wants they cannot stay where they are: to become God's people they have to change and to move.

Moses is anxious about moving and about who will help him in the leadership. Like many of us, Moses would rather not move until he knows he is certain of his supporters (v. 12). The same man has grown in confidence and knows God cares for him; now he asks God to show his care by revealing his plans for the future: 'please show me your ways, so that I can understand you and win your favour' (v. 13). Moses obviously wants to do God's will but is not sure what it is. So often people talk as if God's will was absolutely clear. There is always the danger of saying 'God wants what we want', when we should be saying 'We want what God wants'. Moses reminds God that the Israelites are his people. We need to remember we too are his people. We come from God. We belong to God. We will return to God. 'We are his people and the sheep of his pasture.'

God's reply to Moses is not to give him a map, or even at this stage to offer human resources. God says, 'I myself will go with you, and I will give you rest' (v. 14). God reminds Moses that he is ever present and ever willing to help. God led them out of Egypt; God delivered them from death; God provided them with food in the wilderness; God was with them at Sinai, and God would not leave them or forsake them. We might not know what lies ahead but we know who is there to meet us in each eventuality. We are not left as orphans, we are not left alone: our God goes with us at all times.

Moses says those lovely words to God, 'If you are not going with us yourself, do not make us leave this place' (v. 16). God replies that he knows his friend and he will not forsake him (v. 17). It is good to think over these words.

I said to the man who stood by the gate of the year,
'Give me a light that I may tread safely into the unknown'.
And he replied, 'Go out and put your hand into the hand
    of God,
that shall be to you better than a light,
and safer than a known way.'

(Minnie Louise Hoskins, *Desert*, 1908; quoted by
King George VI in his Christmas Broadcast 1939)

127

FORWARD TO FREEDOM

My dearest Lord,
be a bright flame before me,
a guiding star to lead me,
a smooth path beneath me
and a kindly shepherd behind me,
today, tonight and forever.

(St Columba)

40

The Glory of God

Moses said, 'Show me your glory, I beg you'. • And he said, 'I will let all my splendour pass in front of you, and I will pronounce before you the name Yahweh. I have compassion on whom I will, and I show pity to whom I please. You cannot see my face,' he said 'for man cannot see me and live.' • And Yahweh said, 'Here is a place beside me. You must stand on the rock, • and when my glory passes by, I will put you in a cleft of the rock and shield you with my hand while I pass by. • Then I will take my hand away and you shall see the back of me; but my face is not to be seen.'

Exodus 33:18–23

The cloud covered the Tent of Meeting and the glory of Yahweh filled the tabernacle. • Moses could not enter the Tent of Meeting because of the cloud that rested on it and because of the glory of Yahweh that filled the tabernacle.

At every stage of their journey, whenever the cloud rose from the tabernacle the sons of Israel would resume their march. • If the cloud did not rise, they waited and would not march until it did. • For the cloud of Yahweh rested on the tabernacle by day, and a fire shone within the cloud by night, for all the House of Israel to see. And so it was for every stage of their journey.

Exodus 40:34–38

The more we learn of and enjoy God's love, and the more experience we have of any sort of relationship with him, the more we know there is to learn and experience. In our dealings with God there are always new depths, we are for ever just on the edge of his great glory. The depth and wonder

of God is unfathomable. Though God is far beyond our compre-
hension, he is not beyond our experience or our love: God can
be found and held in our hearts. Many of the saints have taught
that the heart is made for God and it has a capacity for holding
God in love.

Moses longs for a greater awareness. He has seen deeper
into the power and presence of God than many people have,
but this in itself makes him long for more: Moses seeks a vision
of glory (33:18). Our prayer time and times of quiet are only
becoming right when we long for more, when we want more
time in God's presence and love. Though Moses has experienced
the burning bush and the voice on the mountain, though he
has known the power of God in the wilderness, he cannot
live off past experience alone: he longs for a new and deeper
experience; he senses that there is far more to God's glory than
he has ever known. God warns Moses that there are limits to
the human ability to cope with a vision of God in his splendour;
no one can see God and live (33:21). Now God comes as Moses
requests but protects him from the transcendence that would
consume all things. What Moses experienced when he was
sheltered in the cleft of the rock is beyond the power of words
to convey. The glory that is revealed is not a physical shape
but the nature of God – and that is mind-blowing. Goodness
and grace, love and mercy, forgiveness and faithfulness,
power and peace, and much, much more make up the fullness
of God.

God is always willing to meet us if we open our lives to him.
If we seek to see God we will be called to obey him and to
reflect his nature. The word 'glory' is shorthand for all that
God is. The response to glory is worship. Moses bows before
the presence in awe and wonder, in submission and worship.
When Moses bows before the presence it is not another occasion
for collecting facts, it is a deep and moving experience of him
in whom we live and move and have our existence; it is an
experience that will change his life.

When I was at theological college, I was asked to write an essay on 'glory'. I found it hard to put into words what I wanted to write, so I turned to a book that explained biblical words and looked up 'glory': the entry in the book said '(see God)'! I knew that was the answer, so I closed the book. If you want glory in your life you need to become aware of God and of his goodness. I did not find writing the essay any easier, but I did seek to know his glory. St John guides us to the easiest way to behold the glory of God, and that is in the face of our Lord Jesus Christ. The Word was made flesh, he lived among us, and we saw his glory – the glory of the only Son of the Father, full of grace and truth.

The glory of God goes with his people on their journey (40:34–38). The presence never leaves his people; God leads them at every stage of their journey. That glory is with us and about us. The story of the Exodus began with what could have been disaster and ends in glory. Pray that you also come to the glory of God.

> Lord, on the way of goodness,
> when we weaken, strengthen us;
> when we stray, direct us;
> when we stumble, raise us up;
> when we sin, forgive us;
> when we are weary, refresh us.
> Lord, give us all we need for our journey;
> take away all that hinders us from coming to you;
> bring us at the last to the fullness of your glorious
>   kingdom.

Easter Day
Jesus, the Second Moses

The Exodus was the pattern of redemption that the Jews knew and understood: God is a redeeming God who brought his people out of slavery and into the Promised Land. God resued them from death; he fed them with manna in the wilderness; he provided them with life-giving water; he revealed his glory to them. What the Israelites experienced in the wilderness concerning the love and care of God finds its fullness in Jesus Christ. Jesus comes to rescue his people from the slavery of sin and death and to bring them into the glorious liberty of the children of God. Jesus comes to set his people free. Zechariah declares, concerning Jesus, 'Blessed be the Lord, the God of Israel, for he has visited his people, he has come to their rescue . . . to give light to those who live in darkness and the shadow of death, and to guide our feet into the way of peace' (Luke 1:67–79). There is no doubt that the Gospel writers saw Jesus as the one who accomplished the redemption that is greater than that of Moses and delivered his people from a captivity that was stronger than that of Egypt.

On the Mount of Transfiguration, we have a new Sinai; there Jesus is radiant as was Moses (Mark 9:2–8; cp. Exodus 34: 29–35 and 2 Corinthians 4:6). Here God speaks out of the cloud as he did to Moses; the words are much the same as were heard at the baptism of Jesus and earlier spoken to Moses (cp. Deuteronomy 18:15). In rabbinical teaching Elijah was a second Moses, who contended for the Law and encountered God on the holy mountain (1 Kings 19:8). Jesus, in the same way, and with Moses and Elijah, is seen on the 'holy mountain'. Peter wants

132

to make a tabernacle for the presence, like the people of Israel did of old. Already Jesus has also been in the desert for a period of forty days, he has fed people with bread in the wilderness; signs and wonders have been revealed through him: he has come to fulfil the Law and asks for obedience. All is part of the pattern of redemption.

It is no accident that Jesus dies at the time of the Passover: 'he is the lamb of God that takes away the sin of the world'. The Last Supper, with the offering of his body and blood, is set within the Passover. When Jesus says, 'This is my blood, which is shed for you for the forgiveness of sins', he is talking of liberation and freedom. He comes to set us free from sin and death, as God set his people free from Egypt through Moses. What God did in Egypt finds a greater fulfilment in what Jesus does through his death and resurrection.

Rejoice today in our Lord Jesus Christ who has conquered the powers of the Evil One and has brought us into the glorious liberty of the children of God. This Christ was in danger as a child, as Moses was. He spent time in the desert and he heard the voice of the Father. He gathered to himself 'twelve tribes'. His words were accompanied by signs and wonders. He fed people in the wilderness with bread from heaven; he offered life-giving water. He came to fulfil what Moses had done. On the mountain he was transfigured. The final stages of Christ's life show deeply the love and care of God; through him the power of sin and death are conquered, we are given a new liberty. In him we are able to experience the glorious liberty of the children of God: to walk as children of the day and not of the night. In him, who has triumphed over death, we are offered newness of life and life which is eternal.

The Promised Land is offered to us, but we often sit at its borders murmuring and failing to enter into it. New life, eternal life, is God's gift to us, yet we are in danger of living in the shadow of sin and death. We need to have our eyes opened and our faith extended until we see ourselves walking in God's world and doing his will, until we recognise the presence that is always with us, offering us freedom and life eternal. We need to move forward into this new awareness and new life.

> Come to the edge,
> he said. They said:
> We are afraid.
> Come to the edge,
> he said. They came.
> He pushed them,
> and they flew.
>
> (Guillaume Apollinaire, 1880–1918)

Alleluia to our God:
To you, O Christ, for you are risen:
by your death you have conquered death:
By your rising you have opened the way to glory:
Though you entered the desert of darkness and death,
You have opened the Kingdom of Heaven to all believers.
You, Lord, have destroyed the powers of the evil one:
You have freed us from the slavery of sin and death:
You have brought us to the edge of the Promised Land.
Lord, in your risen power, may we rejoice in your kingdom:
serving you, whose service is perfect freedom.
Praise and thanksgiving are yours, radiant Christ:
You have won us the victory. Alleluia.